In God's time

All Bible texts are from the New International Version
except where indicated.

KJV = King James Version
NLT = New Living Translation
NKJV = New King James Version
REB = Revised English Bible

First published 2006
Copyright © 2006

ISBN 1-904685-24-2

Published by
The Stanborough Press Limited,
Alma Park, Grantham, Lincs.

Printed in Thailand

in God's time

Being the best you can be

Andrew Singo

About the author

Kossi Andrew Singo, DipEd, BBA, MAED, MBA, is the Chief Executive Officer of Patts Consultants Ltd, Reading, and of Support Africa International UK (a charity registered in the UK under the name East and Central Africa Education Services).

His specialist subject was Educational Psychology and, prior to taking up his current career, he worked for many years as a teacher.

He was born in Tanzania, and is now lay leader of his congregation at Whitley.

Andrew is happily married and has three children.

Introduction

Almost every Christian has a favourite Bible story that captures his or her imagination more than other stories. Mine is the story of Abraham and his wife Sarah. Although nothing much is told of the couple's childhood, we read that when Abraham was 75 and Sara 66 they moved from where they grew up to a new land that they had never seen before. **'Go to the land that I will show you, . . . and I will make you into a great nation.'** (Genesis 12:1, 2.)

What a joke to an old, childless couple!

Going to an unknown land was not an easy thing to do, considering their ages. For a twenty-year-old couple it might have been a backpacking adventure to travel the world. But for Abraham and Sarah, retired and settled in their home, this was no joke. But in fact it was the voice of God that came to Abraham, asking him to leave his home and go in search of a new land. Few people today would be convinced that such a voice had come from God, and even fewer would take it seriously.

Neither does the story unfold smoothly. Not so much desiring to become a 'great nation', Abraham is actually quite desperate to become a father to *one* child for the first time! His barren wife Sarah resorts to suggesting he should sleep with their Egyptian maid, Hagar. But when Hagar gets pregnant, she scoffs with pride at her mistress and loses all respect for her. More misery for the elderly couple! Hagar is sent away with her son Ishmael, and Abraham does not understand how he can become the father of many nations.

However, on his 99th birthday, Abraham receives another confirmation from God. **'Your wife, Sarah, will bear you a son.'** Sarah laughs, but God confirms it by asking, **'Is there anything too hard for the Lord?'** Abraham looks with disbelief at his wife, only nine years younger than himself. But the Lord assures him that in a year Sarah will bear him a son. Sure enough, Sarah conceives and has a baby boy, and they call him Isaac (21:1, 2).

Sixteen years later God calls again to Abraham. **'Take your only son, and give him to me as a sacrifice.'** What? The son of my old age? Give him as a sacrifice? Are you serious, God? But God is serious. If the Lord had not made Abraham's barren wife fruitful, he would not have had a son at all. So Abraham obeys the command of God, recognising that the boy belongs to God anyway, but it was not any easy thing to do (see Genesis 22).

Abraham travels to Mount Moriah, and builds an altar for the sacrifice. He ties up the young lad, and lays him down on top of the firewood. He looks at the boy for a long time, and breathes a prayer looking up to heaven. Then he raises his knife, ready to cut his son's throat. But right on time, God intervenes again and says, **'Do not lay a hand on the boy.'** Abraham turns, and sees a ram caught by its horns in the thicket behind him.

So Abraham takes the ram and offers it as a sacrifice to the Lord instead of his son. And he calls the place Jehovah-jireh, meaning, 'in the mountain of the Lord it shall be provided' (NKJV). God's timing is always perfect. He has everything you require, at the right place and at the right time.

That is the message of this book. Its theme is the when, where, why, what and who of God's timing. May God bless you as you read its chapters, and it is my belief that you will be able to find the new you in God's time. I also believe that you will discover the potential that God has put in you, waiting to be released.

You are a giant and the sky is the limit.

You are the only You in his time

It was a bright spring morning when I opened the curtains of my bedroom window. Brilliant sunshine flooded into the room. I quickly closed my eyes again, and rubbed them for a few seconds. They were still heavy with sleep. But I took a long, deep yawn and opened the window so that a fresh, cold breeze rushed in and hit my bare chest. I felt refreshed and stretched to tell my body it was time to face another day.

A sparrow flew right up to the window, and looked at me as if to remind me that summer was just one month away, and that other birds would soon be back from Africa and the Mediterranean. The incident brought to my mind the words from Ecclesiastes 3:1-11. 'To every thing there is a season, and a time to every purpose under heaven: A time to be born and a time to die; a time to plant and a time to pluck up that which is planted; . . . A time to get and a time to lose; . . . a time to keep silence and a time to speak; A time to love and a time to hate; . . . What profit hath he that worketh in that wherein he laboureth? . . . He hath made every thing beautiful in his time.' (KJV.)

I went for a shower, and the day's activities started to unfold in my mind. I had planned a busy schedule of visiting customers to sell our services. It was a little mundane, perhaps, but necessary, because my wife and I run our own company. On my way out of the bathroom, towel wrapped around my waist, I passed in front of the mirror and saw how big my belly had grown. Like the mirror belonging to the queen in the famous story of Snow White, my mirror was not going to deceive me. But faced with the truth, I knew I did not have to react as the queen had done.

'Oh Queen, thou art of beauty rare, but Snow White living in the glen is a thousand times more fair.' The words spoken by the magic mirror in the story planted a seed of hatred and jealousy in the heart of the queen, which grew and grew till it blossomed into a plan to murder her rival. The queen's self-esteem dropped low, and finally she was destroyed by her envy and hatred.

That also happened to many a character in the Bible: to the world's first children, Cain and Abel; to Leah and her sister Rachel; to Joseph and his brothers; to King Saul and to little David. And it happens to so many of us today. It seems that each one of us has something that other people want, and each lacks something that other people have. It is tempting to believe that if we have whatever it is we desire we shall be more loved, or more famous, or more worthwhile, or more complete as men and women.

Our fragile self-worth produces a competitive spirit, and a burning envy that eventually destroys our God-given ability to appreciate ourselves and love others. It creates pain, anger, anxiety and stress. It reduces our sense of good and evil, and it tears down the happiness and peace in our hearts, homes and communities.

Most of us are affected by the physical, economic, financial, academic or social success of others. Do you ever feel bad when someone has something you desperately need? Do you ever feel threatened by their success? Do you think of putting that person down because of that success? Do you wish them

In God's time

well or ill? If you feel bad, that is envy, resulting from ignorance and a failure to appreciate who you are in God's eyes.

Envy is defined in the *Chambers English Dictionary* as 'a feeling of hostility, discontent and ill-will because of another's advantages or possessions'. 'A feeling of chagrin at the good looks, qualities, fortunes, of another.' 'To desire with emulation and rivalry what another person has.' Envy both desires the good that you do not have, and despises the good that you have. Envy's cousin is jealousy, which comes from fearing you may lose what you already possess. Both envy and jealousy are the result of a lack of self-esteem.

Larry Litchenwalter says that 'perhaps (envy) might result when we feel empty and unfulfilled because we have not developed good boundaries or taken full responsibility for our lack, or for not doing something about it when we could.'[1]

God has given everyone unique and special qualities and gifts. There are two difficulties. First, to know what those qualities and gifts are. Second, to appreciate them highly enough and give them the value they deserve. Failure to appreciate what God has given you contributes towards envy of others, and that in its turn can end up destroying you. The Bible is full of stories about people who were not satisfied with what they were, or with what they had, and whose envy led them to do regrettable things. The relationship between Laban, Jacob, Leah and Rachel (Genesis 29-33) is a prime example.

Envy focuses on other people, and prevents you from reaching your potential in God's timing. His way focuses on you, and his success is generated from the inside of you. Of course, everyone wants personal prosperity, a cosy home, holidays, material possessions and financial security. But success in God's time means more than worldly goods and a luxurious lifestyle. It includes self-respect, integrity, and personal development in terms of happiness, joy, peace, and satisfaction in relationships

---

1 Larry Litchenwalter, *Wrestling with the Angels*.

and work. God's definition of success means being able to do more for those who depend on you. It is not competitive, and consists of winning without hurting others.

God has set no limit to our personal success. Jesus said that if we work with him, and believe in him, then we shall be able to perform even greater miracles than those that he performed.

Do not fear being yourself

The receptionist at the desk of my first customer that morning fired several questions at me through the intercom system before releasing the door catch to let me in. When she saw me, she was obviously surprised, and asked, 'Are you sure you were invited? I have to ask the manager!'

I intercepted her thoughts with the question, 'Did you expect to see a white man?' The lady was embarrassed and upset because I had read her mind. Very often, in almost all parts of the world, skin colour and speech can determine how quickly and how well you succeed in material terms. Prejudice hurts both sides. It is so easy to suffer low self-esteem and a lack of self-confidence unless you see yourself as special, uniquely created by the God who loves you. And those foolish people who think their colour gives them superiority over others can also be sidetracked from their God-given missions.

The Bible tells us that God made only one Adam and one Eve. We are all descended from them. We have all sinned and fallen short of God's glory. We all need a saviour to bring us back into God's presence, and his grace to live a happy and fulfilled life. **'From one man he made every nation . . . and he determined the times set for them and the exact places where they should live.'**[2] Apart from the natural process, human beings have never been able to create other human beings. Even supposing scientists could go on to produce human clones, they would still need to use cells originally

2 Acts 17:26

In God's time

created by God, passed from human to human through birth. And what scientists are practising now, God did first. After all, Eve was taken from Adam's side. Although Eve was not a clone from Adam, Adam called her **'bone of my bones and flesh of my flesh.'**[3]

You are not who you are by accident

In growing up and mixing with people from different places, we find that our views on life and patterns of belief can change. Whatever we believe, we act out in our attitudes towards others – which can get us into trouble if we are not prepared to face reality. Sometimes we find ourselves at odds with society in our relationships at work or in school. We feel our personal power being challenged when we face those whose beliefs and values are different from the ones we have held for a long time.

Such unpreparedness brings stress, and can cause us to behave badly or out of character. In our own environment we feel we have power over what we do, and have confidence that we are interacting freely as natural hosts. However, when we move to a new environment, we may have to surrender those powers, and change our behaviour in order to fit in. We find ourselves having to submit to new authorities and different customs. It can feel chaotic, artificial and controlling. At its worst, it can leave people feeling discouraged and stressed out.

Our weapon against such discouragement is the development of a physical, mental and spiritual presence *on the inside*. This generates increased confidence, efficiency, and understanding. The Creator has given everyone the ability to learn appropriate attitudes, which lead to an effective and integral use of personal power.

When God created man, he declared him *'Very good'*. In fact, God spent time to create a perfect man, in contrast to the quick *'Let there be'* which he used for the rest of

3 Genesis 2:23

creation. God's purposes and plans for you, and your ultimate success, are greatly thwarted by false perceptions of yourself, and a failure to accept yourself as you are.

If you have this problem, you have damaged your past and you have contributed to the process of dwarfing the future that God wants for you. Even if you have achieved some form of success, it will not be the full potential that God has in store for you. There is no limit for God's people because there is always more room for growth each day. The good news is that it is never too late. Do not let your future be affected by a failure to understand that you are capable of much greater things – just as you are!

Of course, no one is promised a traffic-free highway to his destination, but God promises challenge, followed by victory. Without exams, there can be no graduation. The struggles you endure as you move towards your goal are part of the course work you have to persevere with before you receive your certificate. The apostle Paul says, *'All who run expect a reward.'* It is after running, sweating and enduring aching muscles and chest pains that athletes stand on the podium to hear the national anthem played in honour of their victories.

This is your challenge: accept yourself and respect your God-given abilities to achieve your goals. Help others to make use of their God-given potential. Whoever helps other people to climb, climbs high himself. Love God, because he made you as you are for a purpose and, once you know who you are, you become unstoppable in God's time, in whatever field you desire. Jesus walked ahead, and all you have to do is follow. You do not have to discover a new route, so you will get there in God's time. Remember, you are who you are for a reason.

Personal power

God has made you to be unique

God's creative work has been accomplished with such careful designing, such precision and artistic imagination, that the beauty of his work cannot be hidden. His creative abilities can be seen on the face of every person. However hard you look, you will never find two people the same. Each one has a different shape of lips or nose, a different colour of hair or skin, even a different way of walking. We are **'fearfully and wonderfully made.'**[4] Forensic experts have taken advantage of our uniqueness to convict criminals by using fingerprints. Complicated crimes that have left no trace of fingerprints can sometimes be solved through the use of DNA, which is unique and personal to every individual. God spent time to design each one of us lovingly with his or her own physique, feelings, emotions and intelligence.

'The Lord God formed the man from the dust of the ground and breathed into his nostrils the breath of life, and the man became a living being.'[5] God not only created the outside body; he created the inner being, with an innate sense of self. He gave man the personal power to be a unique individual. That uniqueness cannot be destroyed by other people's opinions. Nor does it depend on what anyone does. A

4 Psalm 139:14
5 Genesis 2:7

true sense of self comes from being in a relationship with the Creator who formed us. God has given us all the personal power to ask for and find all that we need to accomplish well and simply every task he has given us to do.

Your personal power determines how much you like, love and appreciate yourself. It determines the level of your confidence in doing right things at right times, both in daily routines and in moments of crisis. God has given you an ability to listen to comments and criticisms from others without being threatened, so that you can pursue what is valuable and discard what is negative.

Because you are made with love, you have been given the ability to take care of your own needs in order to maintain your energy, and the sense of self worth which enables you to help others. Because God wants you to grow and develop into maturity, he has given you natural personal powers that allow you to make decisions.

Forced away from your true identity

A brief look at society in the 21st century is enough to reveal exactly what happens when the personal powers which people have from the Creator are not valued. Instead of being the men and women that God intended them to be, very many people try to become something that they think will please or impress others.

Professionals are tired, stressed and driven. Pastors are exhausted in trying to live up to the expectations of their congregations. People are controlled by their business partners, managers, neighbours, friends, teachers and spiritual leaders. If your personal power is given away, you cannot even decide what to give your children, how to discipline them and what to teach them. You become mentally and emotionally swamped by the values and beliefs of those you perceive to be your superiors. Your self-esteem goes down as you worry about what others may be thinking of you, and you become a slave to everyone around you. When your personal power is given up, then self doubt, distrust and secret grievances take its place.

When the way you see yourself is derived from what other people think, rather than from what God says about you, then your image of yourself is distorted. It is easy to lose the ability to be yourself, and to stand up for your own values.

Being yourself is the most important starting point for good relationships between you and God, between you and your family, and between you and the rest of society. There can be no environment of peace and harmony as long as people are adopting false identities, and acting out what they imagine they are expected to be.

Honest feedback is important, because the way people look and act, and the way they *think* they look and act, are very different indeed. There is always room for improvement. In my culture there is a saying, 'Do not think the way you have always thought, because if you do so, you will act the way you have always acted and get what you always got.' God has given us the personal power to say no to those things that hinder us from reaching our God-given potential. Even a person with only average self-esteem has enough power to handle criticism, to accept weak areas in his life and to develop. So, no matter what has happened to you in the past, do not allow any pattern of behaviour to bring you down. *You are free to change.*

Liking yourself

It seems there are very many people in the world who have been so hurt emotionally, physically, mentally and spiritually, that they have ended up hating themselves. Some of them know it; others do not seem to know that they don't like themselves. Self-hatred or self-rejection affects not only the victim, but inevitably spreads to include others and causes ripples of relationship problems all around. It is true that hurt people hurt people.

In contrast, God wants us to live happy and fulfilled lives by having good relationships. The apostle Peter tells us to **'seek peace. . . . For the eyes of the Lord are on the righteous and his ears are attentive to their prayer.'**[6] And Jesus says, **'Blessed are the peacemakers, for they will be called sons of God.'**[7]

Peace does not come in a cheap package. You have to pursue it faithfully throughout life, like a soldier acting as part of the peace keeping forces in troubled places in the world. **'Whoever would love life and see good days . . . must seek peace and pursue it.'**[8] Jesus also says, **'Peace I leave with you; my peace I give to you. I do not give to you as the world gives. Do not let your hearts be troubled and do not be afraid.'**[9]

Disliking yourself removes from you the peace that God gives, and it makes you troubled. So the first step to building self-acceptance is to receive the love and peace of God in your heart. Then you can begin to give that love back to God and to the people around you. You cannot give what you do not have. You need to receive it first. **'God has poured out his love into our hearts by the Holy Spirit, whom he has given us.'**[10] When you allow the Holy Spirit of God into your heart, you invite God's love in, and this is what allows you to love him back, and to love yourself, and your fellow human beings.

It is also God's love poured in which makes it possible for you to overcome any bad experiences from your past which may have left you feeling destitute or bereft of love. Nothing is beyond God's redemptive love, even the worst abuse or betrayal from family, friends, trusted neighbours or church leaders. The law of God wants you to love yourself. **'The entire law is**

---

6 1 Peter 3:11, 12   9 John 14:27
7 Matthew 5:9   10 Romans 5:5
8 1 Peter 3:10, 11

summed up in a single command: "love your neighbour as yourself." '[11] It is not possible to love others if you do not first love yourself. Remember, you are the only person you will never be able to get away from. That is why Jesus says, 'Love your neighbour as yourself.'

When you fear that no one loves you, it is easy to end up hating yourself. Many suicides are committed by people who believe that they are unloved. Until you acknowledge the love of God in your heart, the ability to love yourself and others will not be attained. The apostle Paul says, 'For this reason, I kneel before the Father. . . . I pray that out of his glorious riches he may strengthen you with power through his Spirit in your inner being, so that Christ may dwell in your hearts through faith. And I pray that you, being rooted and established in love, may have power, together with all the saints, to grasp how wide and long and high and deep is the love of Christ, and to know this love that surpasses knowledge – that you may be filled to the measure of all the fullness of God.'[12]

This kind of love brings you the fullness of God, and can allow you to love that which God loves. The love of Jesus enables you to love an enemy; to pray for those who devise evil, and to say at the end, 'Forgive them because they don't know what they are doing.' This is the love that can make you accept yourself right now. Know that in God's time, you will be changed and become what he wants you to be.

God's love is patient, kind, and bears with you forever. It will help you slowly but surely to conquer all the sins that destroy your relationships. The Israelites were not established in the Promised Land overnight. They got there bit by bit, and God treats us all just the same. Little by little, he moves us from glory to glory, as we continue to pursue peace with everyone. 'Being confident of this, that he who began a good work

11 Galatians 5:14
12 Ephesians 3:14-19

in you will carry it on to completion until the day of Christ Jesus.'[13]

Conquering fear and insecurity

God has a hard time making people accept that his love really is free. Perhaps as a result of dire warnings from Mum that strangers offering gifts are not to be trusted, there is some suspicion and doubt in most people's minds about God's motives. Rules that are set in childhood to protect us can become a hindrance and are twisted by Satan to keep us in fear and insecurity about God's love. Most people have had bitter experiences that make them suspicious about even the most benign and friendly offers. Gifts from men (and women) very often come with strings attached so that the consequences of accepting them are unacceptable. Many tears have been shed because people have failed to give the love they were supposed to give. Wars are waged and blood shed because men fail to see themselves in the lives of those they kill. They do not have any love to give, so they pour out hatred instead.

Remember that the damage is not always done to us; we, too, have probably hurt people at some point in life and caused grief to them. So we must not waste any more time, but call out, 'Have mercy on me, Lord Jesus.'

The gift of God's love has no strings attached. Jesus said, '**I have come that they may have life, and have it to the full.**'[14] He wants us to live happily, receive his love, live a balanced life, love ourselves, and love him back. Once we receive God's love, we start developing confidence in ourselves; our relationship with him and with our neighbours starts to change for the better.

In God's time, you can learn to accept yourself, even though you may have been guilty of behaving badly in the past. To continue rejecting and despising yourself will never change you for

13 Philippians 1:6
14 John 10:10

In God's time

the better. It will only destroy you. With God's help, as you start to accept yourself the way he accepts you, you receive the power to reason with yourself about what you want to become. You receive the ability to face reality and move on. If God gave his only son, Jesus, to die for you, who are you to say that God's love has no power to bring change into your life?

The greatest enemy of your progress is yourself. If you choose to receive God's love and forgiveness, nobody can stop you. Stop despising the power of God's love in you, and take time instead to appreciate those things that make you special and unique. Remember that God allowed your birth at just the right time, and in the right place. He gave you the right gifts to enable you to fulfil a duty that nobody else can fulfil. God's opinion of you is what matters the most – and he says you are special. **'You saw me before I was born. Every day of my life was recorded in your book. Every moment was laid out before a single day had passed. How precious are your thoughts about me, O God!'**[15]

You are the child of the King of the Universe, so learn to live like one and worry less. Learn to pray to God that he will transform you, establish you and make you strong in understanding yourself and your abilities. You can use this prayer to begin with.

Lord, it has taken me a long time to figure out that I am different by your divine design; that you have made me with abilities, traits and a genetic makeup that nobody else has. Nobody in the whole of history has ever been the person I am – and nobody ever will be. O Lord, save me from feeling weird, and from wishing I were someone else. Save me from envy and jealousy towards others. Help me to discover the unique person you created me to be, and to enjoy the little things that make me special, a one-off creation. Help me realise that I can give the world something that nobody else can give.

15 Psalm 139:16, 17, NLT

The apostle Paul says, **'Be careful, then, how you live . . . making the most of every opportunity.'**[16] Your life has a special mission, right here and now. Where you are is the right place to jump from. In the book *There are No Limits*, Danny Cox puts to us the following arguments. 'The future is nothing more than an approaching series of "nows". During one of them I must make a decision that all future "nows" will be different. A brighter future grows out of a more enlightened and disciplined "now". Therefore my future improves only as I make better use of the current moment.'[17]

Do not blame yourself for your past. Once you have asked God to forgive you, move on, because the time you have left is more important and matters most to God. No matter what others say, be willing and determined from now on to improve your present moments. Life is too short, and today quickly becomes yesterday. But use today, by putting your strengths and abilities back into God's hands, and that way a brighter future will be guaranteed. According to Cox, 'The velocity that carries the present into the past also carries you towards the future, when increasingly, all your goals, or lack of them, will become a reality.'

I made a choice some years ago that I would not stay in my comfort zone. Instead I decided to use all that I had been given to the maximum. God has never suffered from a lack of ideas, right? His greatest difficulty is to get people to act on his ideas. Just look in the Bible at some of the reactions he had. Moses said, 'I am not a gifted speaker.' Gideon's reply to God was, 'I don't have the right connections.' Jeremiah complained, 'I am too young.' What excuse are *you* making up? Whatever it is, remember that God says to all his children, **'I will strengthen you and . . . uphold you with my righteous right hand.'**[18]

There is no better way to end this chapter than by quoting a poem by Russell Kelfer, entitled, 'You are who you are'.

---

16 Ephesians 5:15, 16
17 Danny Cox
18 See Isaiah 41:10

In God's time

You are who you are for a reason.
You are part of an intricate plan
You are a precious and unique design,
Called God's special woman or man.
You look like you look for a reason.
Our God made no mistake.
He knit you together within the womb.
You are just what he wanted to make.
The parents you have were the ones he chose,
And no matter how you may feel,
They were custom-designed
With God's plan in mind,
And they bear the Master's seal.
No — that trauma you faced was not easy.
And God wept that it hurt you, but
It was allowed to shape your heart, so
That into his likeness you'd grow.
You are what you are for a reason.
You have been formed by the Master's rod.
You are what you are, Beloved,
Because there is a God.

Your 'who' against your 'do'

What are you doing? Who asked you to do what you are doing? Have you ever made an analysis of what you are doing, and compared it with the kind of person you are?

There is a Bible story of a boy who became bored with life at home. Most people don't expect to receive their inheritance when their fathers are alive and well, but this boy asked for his money while his dad was fit and healthy. His father understood his younger son's request, and decided to allow him all he asked for. Loaded with money, the boy set off towards a big city.

With his money the boy did everything he wanted to do. He bought whatever he fancied, made new friends and shared his wealth around. He ate and drank as he pleased. Eventually, the money ran out, and the boy, broke and unhappy, found himself with nothing to eat. He looked for a job, but because he was a foreigner in that place he could not get work. Finally, he managed to get a job feeding pigs, and, hungry as he was, he even ate the food that was meant for the animals. If you have any idea what people feed their pigs you will appreciate just how low this young lad had sunk. One morning, he sat down and made an analysis of his life. He asked himself, 'Who am I? What am I doing here? Do I deserve to be here?'

It was this life assessment and his evaluation of his position, compared with his background, his family line, and the person he knew he was meant to be, which brought him to his senses. He made the most important decision for his future. **'I will set out and go back to my father.'**[19] He didn't worry about how he was going to get home, or if he would meet anyone along the way.

Many people live their lives without stopping to take into account who they are and why they are doing what they do. Most people focus more on what they can achieve than on who they are, more on current profit or immediate needs than on the relationship with their Heavenly Father.

What you do today is very important, because you are exchanging your life and future for it – so let it be good!

There is a saying, old but true. When you sow a thought, you will reap an action. If you sow an action, you will reap a habit. If you sow a habit, you will reap a character. And if you sow a character, you will reap a destiny.

Personal inventory

Making an analysis of who you are, and comparing it with what you are doing – that is, your 'who' against your 'do'– is the subject of personal management. It starts with recognising where you came from, then notes what you are currently doing, and moves on to what you are ultimately capable of doing. It expands outwards to include your ability to act, to fight, and to triumph over the things that might hinder your progress. It is a point from which all roads lead to success or failure.

The value you give yourself is the mark of your integrity. If you make yourself cheap, your self-esteem drops and you lose integrity. God created you, and endowed you with a noble character and the ability to decide how to behave well. He gave you power to imagine and power to make independent choices.

19 Luke 15:18

He set a conscience within you so that you would know when you were behaving badly, and self-awareness to monitor your own progress. You are in charge of your own life!

Let's take this step by step. First, understand who you are because of being created by a loving God. This involves recognising your God-given capabilities and accepting that you can live according to godly principles. Second, discover your strengths, and your unique gifts, and develop your vision of what you would like to become in the future. You will need to choose your own way of doing things based on your values. Third, remember that it is important to make a plan in your head before launching into action. And finally, you must exercise your independent will to put your decisions into practice: to live your life according to your own principles, and make things happen according to your plans.

You can monitor your progress and learn to think positively. Count five things you consider to be achievements in what you do, and then give thanks to God who enabled you to do them. Remember that it is God who puts a great idea in your mind, and, like the baby in the womb, it takes time to develop before it is ready for action.

Sometimes pregnancies have to be terminated, and so it is with your plans and ideas. If they fail to develop, then it can be best to wipe them out and start again. But this is not normally the case. It is far more usual for the baby to grow naturally in its own time and, like the pregnant woman, you need to be careful how you feed it. Choose your counsel carefully when taking advice, and feed on the finest food available. Since you are God-created, you deserve the very best. Who you are and what you do are connected.

What drives you?

'What does the worker gain from his toil? . . . I saw that

all labour and all achievement spring from man's envy of his neighbour.'[20]

Among the most common driving forces we experience are materialism, fear, guilt, anger (resentment or grudges) and the need for approval. It is good to question yours, and to choose carefully what you consider to be your purpose in life. If you have no purpose, you are like a ship without a rudder, or an army without a commanding officer. Your purpose is the source of your drive, your control, your guidance and your direction. When you aim at a golf ball, you want it to go at the right speed, for the right distance.

Materialism, or the hunger to own or possess things, can be one of the greatest distractions. It is a force that engrosses most of us. We have such a passion and desire to acquire things that they tend to take over our purposes in life. Materialism comes from the popular belief that possessions can make us happier or more important than others, more secure or even more famous. It is an illusion. The happiness, security and importance that material goods provide do not last. The goods soon wear out or lose their value, or simply become boring, and we are left feeling hungry for new things, or updated versions of the old.

I had an experience of this recently, when I proudly collected my new Peugeot 406 and felt so good driving at 120 mph in the European Car of the Year 2000. I hadn't gone far down the M4, when I was overtaken by a Lexus that cruised past me on the outside and left me feeling I was barely out of first gear. Immediately, I started yearning for a higher performance car. Material possessions never actually make you more important than you were at birth. Your self-worth is not the same as your bank balance. To God, the most valuable things are invisible and therefore cannot be purchased with money so *don't be obsessed with getting more material things but rather* **'seek**

20 Ecclesiastes 3:9, 4:4

first his kingdom and his righteousness, and all these things will be given to you as well.'[21]

In the Bible there is a story of a man called Simon, who was a sorcerer but became a Christian. He wanted to purchase God's healing powers. When the apostles Peter and John went to Samaria, they laid hands on people to enable them to receive the gift of the Holy Spirit. Simon offered them some money, saying, **'Give me also this ability so that everyone on whom I lay my hands may receive the Holy Spirit.'** Peter answered, **'May your money perish with you, because you thought you could buy the gift of God with money!'**[22]

The things that really make us more important, more secure and happy, are invisible, and cannot be purchased because they come from God. (Love, integrity, grace, hope and faith, for example.) By clinging to possessions, and struggling to fill our lives with worldly, perishable goods, we are sinfully distorting God's plans for us to live eternally with him. Understand that what you are doing now is just a rehearsal for what you will do in Heaven. When you choose your actions carefully, your duties and relationships will help to make you ready for eternity. Grasping the truth of this tends to shake up all your previous ideas, so that you re-evaluate the goals, activities and tasks that you thought important. What was once a big problem becomes something that is not worth worrying about. The closer you are to God, the more this happens. As the apostle Paul says, **'I once thought all these things were so very important, but now I consider them worthless because of what Christ has done.'**[23]

Don't wait until you are on your deathbed to start thinking about eternity, because it will be too late and too painful. It is very foolish indeed to go through life without preparing for what is inevitable. Each new day, you need to plan and think about the hereafter, because every day brings you closer to

21 See Hebrews 13:5 and Matthew 6:33
22 Acts 8:14-20
23 Philippians 3:7, NLT

your time of departure from this world. And your success depends on discovering who you are, and who designed you and created you to do what you are doing. Just as God designed pregnancy to last nine months so that the baby has time to grow and prepare for life on earth, so he gives us life in order that we might grow and prepare for eternity. What you do today influences where you will spend eternity, and there are only two choices. Every moment spent in our earthly bodies is time spent away from our eternal home. And every action prepares us for it, one way or the other. Whatever you do, let it prepare you for good.

From which angle do you see life?

I asked a congregation a very simple question: 'How do you view your life?' I got as many answers as the number of people. Some said life is a game. Some said a race, a circus, a journey, a roller coaster, and many other things. One old man whom I shall always remember said, 'Life is a stream of misery and crumbs of joy.'

Another time, I asked a group of people, 'What is your metaphor for life?' Again there were diverse answers. Some said life is a maze and others said it is an ocean where we fight for life. What you believe life to be like will consciously or unconsciously influence your behaviour on a daily basis. Your metaphor for life not only determines your values, expectations, priorities, aspirations and goals, but, even more importantly, it determines your relationships. For instance, in the case of a young person whose metaphor for life is a party, the primary focus will be having fun, and that person may strive always to be doing things that result in enjoyment and easy living.

The Bible tells us to pick our metaphor carefully. **'Do not conform any longer to the pattern of this world, but be transformed by the renewing of your mind. Then you will** be able to test and approve what God's will is – his good, pleasing and perfect will.'[24]

In three different ways, God has given us pictures and metaphors that emphasise that life is a temporary assignment, a test and a trust. These can help us tackle problems and form a starting point for our plans and actions.

Life as a trust

If you take life as a trust, you will act as a steward or manager, appointed by God to manage the things entrusted to you. Jesus gave a metaphor of life as a trust in the parable of the talents. In the story, the master gave talents to his servants, and went away, leaving them to decide what to do. On his return, the master made performance analyses of all the servants, and rewarded them accordingly. To two of them he said, **'Well done, good and faithful servant. You have been faithful with a few things; . . . Come and share your master's happiness!'** To the third, who had wasted his talents by hiding them, the master showed his displeasure.

The same will apply to every one of us. At the end of our lives, and indeed on the day of judgement, we shall hear, **'Well done, good and faithful servant'** or **'Throw that worthless servant outside into the darkness, where there will be weeping and gnashing of teeth.'**[25]

If God has trusted you with something as valuable as yourself, your children, and all his creation, you ought to show you are worthy of that trust. **'What do you have that God hasn't given you? And if all you have is from God, why boast as though you have accomplished something on your own?'**[26]

Life as a test

Throughout life we have tests and exams to pass, and the time spent in preparation is valuable. But God allows the whole of

24 Romans 12:2
25 Matthew 25:14-30
26 1 Corinthians 4:7, NLT

life to be used in preparation for his testing. I want you to look again into your life and assess what you are doing. Why are you doing it? Who asked you to do it? Remember, **'From everyone who has been given much, much will be demanded; and from the one who has been entrusted with much, much more will be asked.'**[27] If you pass the test of faithfulness to God, then he will reward you with greater opportunities.

Life as a temporary stage

The Bible uses words like pilgrims, strangers, foreigners, aliens, travellers, and visitors, to mean that we are not permanently resident in the world. Compared to eternity, we might say that we live here on earth for only a few minutes. **'For we were born only yesterday and know nothing, and our days on earth are but a shadow.'**[28] However, that does not mean we can afford to be slackers.

I remember at one stage in my life, after I finished my O-Levels, I worked as a temporary field numerator for the World Bank water project in Tanzania. Despite being a temp, I was still held accountable for the assignments I was given. The same applies to our lives. God gives us work to do, and it is only profitable if undertaken with the understanding that it is preparing us for another existence later. Peter says, **'Since you call on a Father who judges each man's work impartially, live your lives as strangers here in reverent fear.'**[29]

The closer we get to the end of the history of this world, the more the world seems to offer attractive lifestyles that pull us away from God. Material possessions, all kinds of entertainments, sports, television programmes, scientific and technological discoveries, work together to divert our attention and seem to demand our involvement day and night. Higher standards of living and many modern luxuries keep us yearning for more money, forcing us to work longer hours, researching new invest-

27 Luke 12:48
28 Job 8:9
29 1 Peter 1:17

ments, and even employing illegal means to gain money to satisfy our egos. These are dangerous times, and many people forget who they are, and lose track of their eternal destiny.

Listen to what God says, **'All these** [great men and women] **were still living by faith when they died. . . . they admitted that they were aliens and strangers on earth. People who say such things show that they are looking for a country of their own. . . . They were longing for a better country – a heavenly one.'**[30]

In other words, God wants us to join the honours list along with Abraham, Moses, Job, Rehab, Peter, Paul, John the Baptist, King David, Daniel, and many others. So the question to ask ourselves is 'whose work are we doing?' If we can concentrate on the unseen things, rather than on the visible things in the world, we shall be able to prepare for something better than this life.

30 Hebrews 11:13-16

Believing in your capabilities

It takes time to grow to reach your true potential. It takes at least fourteen years for the average person, starting school at the age of five, to climb the education ladder to degree level, and possibly three more for the same person to achieve a professional qualification. That is just formal education. In addition, more knowledge and skills are acquired informally along the way from other sources, as part of the process of growing to reach maturity. The human mind and body have an amazing capability, but need nurturing slowly to achieve full potential.

You can see how foolish it is to underestimate the capacity of the human mind when you think of human achievements. Think of the Euro tunnel connecting Britain to France under the sea, or stare up at the moon and remember that human feet have walked on it. It is amazing when you remember Concorde flying across the Atlantic in under four hours. In Genesis it is recorded that God looked down on the human beings he had created who at that time were busy building a giant tower, and he said, **'Nothing they plan to do will be impossible for them.'**[31] God gave mankind limitless potential.

Jesus said that the Kingdom of Heaven could be likened to a man preparing for a journey to a foreign country. The man (God) called his servants and committed all his investments to them. To one, he gave five 'talents', to another two, and to a

31 Genesis 11:6

third he gave one 'talent'. Then he went away on his journey, and left the servants to do the very best they could with what had been entrusted to them. We all have unique abilities, and it is up to us to use them fully, to further God's work on earth, and become successful in whatever we choose during the short period of time we are living in this world.

You have great mental capabilities

Human beings have millions of brain cells, and studies show that the average brain can store up to 100 trillion facts. It can be used to handle up to 15,000 decisions a second. But, like athletes preparing for a race, our mental faculties need training. God has designed our mental powers so well that it is possible to become well informed and efficient in everything our hands find to do. The human intellect is higher than that of animals, so we are enabled to make right choices and decisions. We can choose to put our own selfish desires aside, and to participate in the divine nature as we were created to do, so that we are of value in the service of God.

Our brains have the ability to create things, to imagine, and to store and retrieve information at will. If this is so for the average person, how much more efficient, effective and successful are those whose intellect is placed under the influence and direction of the Creator God, through his Spirit? Ellen White says, 'Let the youth who need an education set to work with a determination to obtain it. Do not wait for an opening; make one for yourselves. Take hold in any small way that presents itself.'

Mrs White continues: 'Be determined to become as useful and efficient as God calls you to be. Be thorough and faithful in whatever you undertake. Procure every advantage within your reach for strengthening the intellect. . . .Through the study of his word, their mental powers will be aroused to earnest activity. There will be an expansion and development of the faculties, and the mind will acquire power and efficiency. Self-discipline must be practised by everyone who will be a worker for God. This will accomplish more than eloquence or the most brilliant talents. An ordinary mind, well disciplined, will accomplish more and higher work than will the most educated mind and the greatest talent without self-control.' (*Christ's Object Lessons*, pages 334, 335.)

God designed us to be unique and with no duplicates! No one on earth will ever have the ability to make the unique contribution to the world that you make, and no one else is performing your role. In addition to your natural talents, there is supernatural power available for those who choose to become Christians. The gift of the Holy Spirit is given freely to those who receive the love of Jesus in their hearts, and submit their lives to the will of God. So much more can be accomplished if you are willing to enter into relationship with God, and talk to him continually. He offers an even higher training, for even better service.

You have great physical capabilities

Your body is built on a skeletal framework of bones, supporting and protecting muscles, blood vessels, nerves and vital organs. The detail in the design is amazing. The Bible tells us we are 'fearfully and wonderfully made'. And human beings have an outstanding ability to push their physical limitations to extremes, as a quick glance at any sporting event will prove. From weight lifting to marathon running, from high jump to high dive, the human body under control after training is magnificent. Even feats of survival cover every field, from the Arctic explorer in extreme temperatures, to David Blain in his self-imposed incarceration in a cage suspended over the Thames for forty-four days without food.

On the other hand, this same human body can be totally disabled by a small problem. A splinter or thorn embedded in your foot can make you inactive for days. Something as small as a microscopic virus can cause harm to the body, to the point of death. So you have a responsibility to look after the body you were given. God wants you to co-operate with him in keeping your body healthy. He wants you to eat and drink properly, and to breathe clean air. God loves our bodies so much he has chosen them to be his home, the place where he wants to live, and a temple of the Holy Spirit. By keeping yourself clean and healthy you make yourself fit for God to live in you.

God's purposes in your life will be greatly affected by the care or negligence of your body. Body care is important. You need to pay attention not only to the way you eat and drink, but the air you breathe as well. Avoid all toxins, poisons, and drug and alcohol abuses which can cause chemical changes to the brain and cause damage to your system. Give love, care and nurture to the outside of your body as well, in washing, drying, dressing and personal grooming. Your appearance can make a difference both to the way you feel inside, boosting your self-confidence, and to the way others see you and the impression you create wherever you go. So take the time and care to dress appropriately according to the event, culture and climate. It is perfectly possible to be fashionable and contemporary in your dressing, while sticking to your Christian values and principles. So, before you leave the house, make sure you are satisfied with your looks. The confidence you gain will help you make and keep friends and acquaintances, and lead you to a full social life.

Personal hygiene is very important to your success at all times. Bad breath or unpleasant body odour can lead people to avoid you. Lack of care in washing can result in skin infections and rashes, bowel and bladder disorders, dandruff and scalp conditions that may be hard to remove. Pay attention to your hair, nails, and teeth. Men should take care to groom their beards or shave regularly. Women need to be particularly aware of hygiene during menstruation. Keep yourself clean and presentable both before the Lord and in your daily walk with others.

It is fine to be open to ideas and to listen to other people's opinions. But remember, God never created less than a first class person, so it is important to place most emphasis on what God says about you, rather than being a people-pleaser. Inevitably you will reveal to others what you really think about yourself, so listen to the truth of what God says about you and then choose to reflect that in your appearance. Above all, be yourself. If you believe in happiness, then talk about happiness; if you believe in progress, talk about progress; if you believe in prosperity, talk about prosperity. Your integrity will be visible when the inside of you matches the outside.

Negligence or indulgence in any area may result in failure to become what you were meant to be in God's time. But with discipline, your mental and physical abilities will produce the right balance for emotional peace, and you will become an instrument worthy of service to God.

You have great emotional capability

God created us with emotions as well. Emotions are not only strange feelings but also complex. They are naturally intense, demand a lot, and they are personal. At times I may feel apprehensive, or I may feel confident, and yet it may be an untrue reflection of what I am logically feeling in the circumstance I am in. I tried to find out what emotions really were. They are generated by apparently more primitive areas of the brain and thereby may be thought of as being internal sensations. The opposite of emotion is the feeling of touch, of warmth, heat or coldness, of pain caused by external sources. Emotions are much more related to conditions in the brain. They reflect the type and degree of mental activity going on in there.

Experts think that fear is the most primitive emotion. What happens when a fierce animal is rushing towards you is most probably the best way of explaining what fear is. You don't plan to become fearful, neither do you call a committee to decide to be fearful. If something bad happened to you in the past, the thought of the situation may bring back painful memories which may cause fear in you.

If you want to be emotionally stable, you must care for your emotions. It is important that you learn to be happy, to be joyful, to be sorrowful, to weep at the right time and in the right place. It would be very abnormal to crack up with laughter at a funeral service. On the other hand it would be madness to weep at a wedding reception unless you were crying for joy. That is why Solomon says in Ecclesiastes, 'there is a time for everything under the sun.' Failure to control your emotions properly results in depression. Depressed persons should be enabled and encouraged so that they may feel supported enough to get over their sadness.

In most cultures, men do not cry in public. This destroys many of them, especially when bereaved of a close family member. Failing to come to terms with their emotions, they repress those feelings and, instead of letting them out at the right time, they bury them only to have them come out or manifest themselves at a later time, perhaps as a depression or as something else more dangerous. If you suppress your grief, by the time you grieve there may be no one to support you, or to be sympathetic with you.

King David, faced by the death of his son, cried and wailed in public. In Italy, in many African tribes, and in Israel, death in a family is followed by shouts, screams, and wailings, and a kind of a public show of sadness, grief, and sorrowfulness, which releases deeply-felt emotions and dissipates them.

In God's time

Instead of keeping a stiff upper lip, it is better for you to laugh, or cry, or let your despair, fears, anxieties, and sadness disappear at the right time. Let all joy flood out when it is the right moment to do so. In so doing, you become emotionally liberated. Jesus did not want to dwell in the emotions of the past. While in pain at the cross, he cried, 'Father, forgive them for they know not what they are doing.'

Your emotional stability can be enhanced through prayer, because prayer can unlock in the heart all the secret chambers that jeopardise your success and can make things work faster than any kind of human means of psychotherapy or psychoanalysis. Far more important is the fact that you do not have to pay anything. Prayer is free.

You have great spiritual capability

When you read the Bible, try visualising and transposing to the present time the events you read about. What happened in biblical times is exactly the same as what happens today, in every street and every city in the world. There are millions of people with bad health, and without food. Thousands suffer terminal illnesses and millions die without help each week. Far too many people in the world today have an experience of life which consists of nothing but the horror of war, loneliness or imprisonment, the agony of torture, hunger or some form of abuse.

If you are a Christian living in the West, and can attend church without any threat, then thank God. Billions of people have never been inside a church. Furthermore, if you have a Bible, you are better off than more than 1.5 billion people who have never seen one. Make the most of all that you have been given. There is no better privilege than to know God, and his son, Jesus, who was sent to redeem us. 'He who has the Son has life.' By accepting Jesus into your life, and choosing to believe that you are a child of God, you make Christ your brother. You have accessed the greatest power in heaven and earth, found in the name of Jesus.

'Be careful how you live, not as fools but as those who are wise.'[32] The Bible also says, 'Do not be carried away by the errors of these wicked people. I don't want you to lose your own secure footing.'[33] The best way to balance your God-given capabilities is always to 'test yourself to make sure you are solid in the faith. Don't drift along, taking everything for granted. . . . Test it out. If you fail the test, do something about it.'[34]

God is a spirit and those who worship him should worship him in spirit. Because we are created in the image of God after his likeness, we are spiritual in nature. The only obstacle is that Satan tries to take away humanity's spiritual powers. That is why, as much as he can, he would like to distract us when we read the Bible because it is a tool to build up our spirituality. When our minds are occupied with commonplace matters more than godly matters, our minds and spiritual powers become dwarfed and enfeebled. The Bible is the central pillar where the redemption plans and the restoration of God's image in the human soul is supported. 'The words that I speak to you,' said Jesus, 'are spirit, and they are life.' He further says, 'This is eternal life, that they may know You, the only true God, and Jesus Christ whom You have sent.' (John 6:63, 17:3, NKJV.)

Ellen White says, 'The creative energy that called the worlds into existence is in the word of God. This word imparts power; it begets life. Every command is a promise; accepted by the will, received into the soul, it brings with it the life of the Infinite One. It transforms the nature and re-creates the soul in the image of God.'[35] Every one of us has a power to choose the type of spirituality to have. Human mind and soul is built up by

32 Ephesians 5:15, NLT
33 2 Peter 3:17, NLT
34 2 Corinthians 13:5, The Message
35 Ellen G. White, *Education*, page 126.

those things that we feed to them; and it rests with each one of us to determine and choose the topics to occupy our minds and to shape the character.

The more we allow the Spirit of God into our lives, the more spiritual power we shall harness. If through the word of God we live in fellowship with heaven, we shall have companionship with angels of heaven. We shall be able to meditate upon those things that **'even angels long to look into.'** (1 Peter 1:12)

Even greater capabilities

Have you ever watched ants at work, collecting and storing their food? They are among the most fascinating of God's creatures and present excellent role models for us. Ants cut pieces bigger than they are themselves. They carry a load greater than their own body weight. And they are very successful. Success belongs to those who carry too big a load, without complaining, in the belief that they can succeed. Success is for those who are too stubborn to leave it behind, and, when it doesn't come, they go after it. The success of ants, indeed the success of the most successful person you know, is rooted in a definite aim. Anyone who wants true success in life must work hard to keep in view the aim worthy of his endeavour.

I remember about five years ago I was in a friend's office. His brother came in and started complaining that he was broke and had no job. My friend asked him a question, 'John, you have just graduated with a Master's degree in Business Administration (MBA) — and you are jobless? I thought a person with an MBA was supposed to create jobs for others, not just look for jobs for himself?' We all laughed, but that was a big challenge to me, too, because I was in the same shoes, having just graduated with an MBA in finance. If God the Creator lives in you through the Holy Spirit, it means that you have the power to create. If you can't find a job, you can create one not only for yourself, but also for others who do not have one.

Someone once asked, 'What is the secret of success?' An old man answered, 'There are many things, but the one thing I think is very important is making good decisions.' 'Well, OK. So how do you learn to make good decisions?' the questioner went on. 'By making bad ones,' he said. The only trouble with many of us is that we are overcautious. A little success takes to a point of 'no more beyond'. True success has no limit because the human mind is growing continuously.

Steering the road towards success involves monitoring our decisions, learning from the results, and being flexible and quick to implement change when we discover we have made a bad decision. Many of the worst pitfalls can be avoided by being careful to abide by God's laws. He made them for our good, and we ignore them at our peril. The consequences of making a decision in violation of God's rules of the game can be at best damaging and at worst irreversible.

Once you know your capabilities and have developed your dreams and discovered your gifts, don't waste time waiting for the so-called 'right opportunities' to fall into your lap. If you use your God-given gifts, then opportunity is the strength of your mind and the breath in your body. No one should tell you what you can or can't do, because you are created to act, and to be a creator yourself. Every opportunity in this world is within your reach, but you have to search for it. Search from every angle, using all the tools around you to get started.

Wealth capabilities

God does not give you money, because he did not make money. However, he has given you the power and ability to make money and to become wealthy (Haggai 2:8). There is a world of difference between the two. The wealth that God gives you lies hidden and dormant until you choose to pick it up and use it. The hopes, the dreams, and the visions, together with your God-given power and abilities, will all amount to nothing if you ignore them. God gives you power to succeed, but it functions only when you are active. So develop a plan; write it down. Communicate it to another person if you need to, and work at it.

Deuteronomy 8:18 says that it is God who gives people the ability to produce wealth. Every human being is created in God's likeness, and has been endowed with the potential to become what God wants him to be, for his work, for his purposes. We are in the world not just for our own benefit, but also for others' benefit.

Zig Zigler says, 'Those who help others to climb, climb higher themselves.' When you work to benefit those around you, not just for your own personal gain, then you receive blessings from the Creator. There is a reference in 1 Chronicles 4:9 to a man called Jabez, one of the unsung heroes of the Bible. Jabez stands as an important role model. He is recorded as being 'more honourable than his brothers', and when he prayed for his territory to be enlarged, God answered and increased his wealth. God does not bless selfishness or greed, but he blesses those who are honourable, and have concern for others.

There is some confusion, even among believers, about whether God gives wealth. Many people have been led to believe that being wealthy is sinful, and as a consequence they do not believe that the blessing of wealth can come through prayer, faith and effort. But the truth is that everything God created he made available to us for our use, and we can choose to use anything wisely for his glory. We are blessed if we use the creation to benefit others, and ourselves, and to better the environment. The Bible says that God's blessings bring wealth (Proverbs 10:22), and that he delights in seeing every one of us succeed (Psalm 35:27). He teaches us how to live (Isaiah

In God's time

48:17). He multiplies what we invest (2 Corinthians 9:6) and gives us things to enjoy (1 Timothy 6:17). 'Till the earth and subdue it' was his instruction to Adam.

Bruce Wilkinson, in *The Prayer of Jabez*, says that the world needs a new definition of the word 'bless'. People have come to understand the word only as a trite expression of sympathy when someone sneezes, or a way of saying thanks before tucking into a meal. But this kind of thinking diminishes our ability to receive from God. When God blessed Abraham, he not only made him a successful businessman, but also an unselfish and faithful person. Blessings from God reach right into the heart, so when God blesses you, no one will be able to stand in your way, even if you had previously been written off as a failure. The Bible is full of stories about the way God's blessings transformed lives. There was David, once a fugitive hiding in caves, who ended up as a king living in a palace. Joseph was sold into slavery by his jealous half brothers, falsely accused of rape and sent to prison, but he became one of the most respected men in Egypt.

'Oh, that you would bless me indeed', should be every man's prayer because God is still in the business of blessing people, just the way he did in biblical times. God will never turn you down, and there can be no doubt that whatever you have will be multiplied — if you commit everything God has given you to his service and his glory. If you are a farmer, then pray, 'Lord, please give me a bumper crop.' If you are a family man, it is good to ask God to give you family resources to impact the community for good. If you are a businessman, it is right to pray, 'Lord, increase my business.' God is surely waiting for you to ask, because he is longing to hear from those who want him to do more.

'You do not have, because you do not ask God.'[36] By asking, you allow God to release to you what is already there for

---

36 James 4:2

you. And by not asking, you forfeit it all. Remember, God speaks of himself as **'abounding in love and faithfulness'**.[37] It is high time to start thinking of God that way, so ask him every morning and evening to bless you, and not just a little but a lot. God gives in full measure, not in halves. Jesus said that if he makes you free, then you will be 'free indeed', meaning completely and utterly free.

Let's look at this as if it were an equation. By the time they have been through school, university or employment training, many people have adopted the belief that destiny = education + skills + capital + appearance + lucky breaks. That is the way our culture appears to work. But now see how it looks from the point of view of a Christian, someone who has committed everything to God. Destiny = one's own inability and lack of resources + God's infinite ability and power. Follow this formula and your territory will be increased. It does not matter what you are engaged in, as long as you do not move away from God's will in anything that you are involved with. Have you ever thought about the healing miracles that Jesus performed? Most of them were initiated by a bold request, a heart cry. When you call out to the Lord, 'Enlarge my territory!' he provides everything you need to fulfil his purposes. He seats you in the driver's seat and places your hands on the steering wheel. When he has done that, it is your responsibility to drive!

There are dangers in all this, of course. To have the benefit of all God's blessings can send you driving straight into disaster, unless you act wisely. God's plan for you is not to put you on the big screen so that people can see your greatness. Rather, he puts you on the big screen so that people can see your humility and his greatness through you. If your riches increase, then don't let it go to your head – or as the Bible says, **'Do not set your heart on them.'**[38] Remember to keep depending on God. You may end up with more business than you can han-

37 Exodus 34:6
38 Psalm 62:10

dle, more opportunities than you can respond to, more calls on your time and talent than you can fulfil. And this may be his way of testing to see if you are able to continue putting first things first – dependence on him before your own activity. **'The eyes of the Lord range throughout the earth to strengthen those whose hearts are fully committed to him.'**[39] God is your support system, if you want him to be. Actually, he is looking for people he can trust with his wealth blessings.

Success can be as dangerous as its opposite, and Jabez showed his wisdom in praying that when he was successful, God would keep him from harm and from causing pain.[40] Perhaps one reason why so many Christians are not rich is that God knows human beings too well. He can see that many people would not use the riches he might entrust to them for his glory, so he keeps them less well off and away from temptation. You may have noticed that one quarter of the Lord's Prayer is about protection. Jesus surely knows how easy it is for human beings to squander wealth, and abuse the blessings of God. The apostle Paul says, **'not that we think we can do anything of lasting value by ourselves. Our only power and success come from God.'**[41]

Being rich is not, in itself, a danger. But what you do after becoming rich can lead you into danger. Did you know that David was in trouble more often after he became a king than when he was a shepherd and a servant? That King Solomon became more foolish the richer he grew? So, however much you receive, keep on giving it all back to the Lord, for his purposes, his plans, and not your own. If you are working for the government, for instance, be ambitious and faithful to God, like Daniel. Be a faithful statesman, a man who cannot be corrupted by money, silver or gold. Even if you have made mistakes in the past, you are capable of saying 'sorry', and turning defeat into victory. By doing so, you do not allow evil to control you,

39 2 Chronicles 16:9
40 See 1 Chronicles 4:10
41 2 Corinthians 3:5, NLT

and you honour your Redeemer.

God's blessings bring power and supernatural favour to every aspect of life, and by submerging your will in his, you will increase the blessings and your success. If you are tired of settling for second best, you can take the opportunity now, and exchange your lack for God's provision. But the warnings are clear. No man is a match for the devil, and it is foolish to think that others have stumbled only because they were less clever than you are. Remember that capabilities for acquiring wealth are based on the providence of God the creator as the original proprietor, while we are just stewards receiving directives from him. With this in mind, you might like to consider joining with a group of like-minded people who understand the ways of God and who will help you to keep your relationship with him as your Number 1 priority. There are others around who believe that God is sovereign, that he chooses how and when to bless people in response to their prayers, and when they are ready to handle still greater blessings. Joining up with some friends can be a great encouragement, and will help you over a period of time to believe that no force can stand in your way when you pray according to God's will. This kind of friendship forms part of God's blessing for you, part of the way he provides for your needs. The only person who can stop you receiving such a blessing is yourself. **'He who walks with the wise grows wise.'** (Proverbs 13:20, NKJV)

I have discovered for myself that it is God's nature, desire and will to bless if I ask. I have learned to keep on asking until I receive, or until I establish that it is not his will to give it to me at that particular time. My hope is that, like me, you will want to take the prayer of Jabez as your own, and call on the God of Israel, saying, **'Oh, that you would bless me and enlarge my territory! Let your hand be with me, and keep me from harm so that I will be free from pain.'**[42] In the same way that

---

42 1 Chronicles 4:10

In God's time

God granted Jabez his request, he has given me what I need, and will continue to supply all my needs. **'Taste and see that the Lord is good.'**[43]

In the time he has allotted for you on earth, God wants you to accomplish a great deal. He has chosen you, not because you are the only person for the job but because through an established connection with him you 'can do all things'. God accepts your offer to serve him if you are determined to aim high. Your only obligation is to be and to do your very best, and then leave the rest to him.

Your best will consist of upholding high Christian standards of behaviour, aiming at moral perfection, developing every capability you have been given, and strengthening your character. Noble characters are not achieved easily or without individual effort by the grace of Christ. **'When he ascended on high, he led captives in his train, and gave gifts to men.'**[44] This means that all those things you cannot do by yourself, he can do for you. Every undesirable character trait, whether inherited or acquired, can be subdued in the name of Jesus. Willing and determined men have the benefit of heavenly messengers to work with them, to change and mould their characters to match the divine likeness; so that finally, in God's time, whatever you do (at his command) will be accomplished through his almighty power.

Through Christ's death on the cross, every human being has been bought at great price, the price of his blood, not silver or gold. God has bought our will, our affections, our bodies and our minds. Christ paid that price and he owned us even before we knew him, whether we believe it or not. But when we choose to accept that truth, we realise that God has a ministry of service for each one of us, towards God and towards our fellow human beings, which connects and binds us together with love. It is when we recognise and accept what Christ did for us

43 Psalm 34:8
44 Ephesians 4:8

that we willingly become his servants. Whether we have one talent or five talents, we have a place in God's eternal plan. Then when we become rich, our riches are for God's purposes, to share with our fellow human beings.

Communication powers

Among the many gifts that God has given us for his service is the ability to speak. Not only can we talk to one another, but we can praise, sing, manipulate, persuade, rebuke, curse, and pray. The voice is ours to use for good or evil as we choose. Let us not forget that the devil managed to trick Eve because of his ability to talk. Often our powers of speech are not cultivated, and we fail to make the best use of them. However, the Bible instructs us to develop this gift, as with all others. **'They read from the Book of the Law of God, making it clear and giving the meaning so that the people could understand what was being read.'**[45] Ezra encouraged the people of his time to read the Law of God distinctly, to give it meaning and to increase understanding among the people. When we speak of and about God we should show clarity and knowledge that brings truth home to doubting hearts.

In addition, we have a responsibility to receive grace onto our lips, so that we can **'speak a word in season to him who is weary'.**[46] It is our duty always to speak with grace (Colossians 4:6), and to minister grace to our hearers (Ephesians 4:29).

If it becomes appropriate to correct somebody, then it is important to be careful with the words you choose. The tone of voice and pitch you pick can either hurt and damage or bless and encourage, and corrective words are best received if they offer healing to wounded souls. Evil speaking, slander, frivolous talk, sinful suggestions and ill-considered advice need to be avoided if you are to allow your power of speech to work towards God's plan for your life. The apostle Paul warns us,

45 Nehemiah 8:8
46 Isaiah 50:4, NKJV

In God's time

'Let no corrupt communication proceed out of your mouth' because 'death and life are in the power of the tongue.'[47]

In presenting yourself to others, always remember that you are an important person. Accept and value yourself as a child of God, and in that way others will be more inclined to respect and value you. Be aware of your own positive qualities, and don't be shy in describing yourself in a good light. If you believe you are special, then you will think and sound confident and happy. Your controlled thinking is part of bringing success into your life in God's time, because 'He hath made every thing beautiful in his time.' (Ecclesiastes 3:11, KJV.)

Anyone who contemplates being successful in God's time must aim at the harmonious development of all his faculties. Avoid a disposition that pushes you to restrict your study and growth to areas that you like or think are naturally to your advantage. Try as much as you can in God's help to aim at simplicity and effectiveness. As all their capabilities are employed in a wise manner, in God's service and in reaching others for him, men and women will produce the best results in life's responsibilities charged on them by the heavens and strive to send to the world messages of hope and courage.

Bless others with what God has blessed you. Let your mouth issue words that encourage and build others. Sow seeds of righteousness in such a way that – even when you are in your grave – others will reap blessed harvests. Be pleased and content with the thought that what you are doing today will last and that you have collaborated with heaven to set in motion an agency of good. Always remember that in heaven all that you do now will be seen and rewarded.

Let me finish this chapter with one of the best comments from Ellen G. White: 'The life on earth is the beginning of the life in heaven; education on earth is an initiation into the

---

47 Ephesians 4:29, KJV; Proverbs 18:21, NKJV

principles of heaven; the life here is a training for lifework there. What we are now, in character and holy service, is the sure foreshadowing of what we shall be.'[48]

---

48 E. G. White, *Education*, page 307

6
With no change inside

There is a lovely story about a little boy who went to church with his mother one Sunday morning. Just as most little boys do when bored, this one kept standing up at the wrong time, and every now and then his mother would say, 'Sit down, son!' Finally her patience snapped and she said in a stern voice, 'Sit down NOW, or you will be in big trouble!' A bit scared, the boy nevertheless replied, 'Well, all right, Mum, I will sit down. But I'm still going to be standing up on the inside!'

Compare this story to something that happened while I was present at a meeting in my local village. There was a man who wanted to address the committee, and kept trying to make his point. But every time he tried, the chairman asked him to sit down again, and to wait until he was called before speaking. Eventually, the man grew exasperated and called out, 'I won't sit down any more, and I insist on making my point.' Indeed, he didn't sit down again until everyone had been made to listen to what he had to say.

There comes a time when you have to decide whether you are going to suffer in silence like a child, or stand up and speak out, even if it means disturbing people in a way they dislike. There may be friends, relatives, neighbours, parents, teachers or bosses who try to stop you from making waves of change, preferring you to remain unnoticed and unheard. It can seem as if they just want you to follow them, to do as you are told like a child. The temptation under these circumstances is to forget your vision and submerge your ideas into their system, to become one of the crowd.

Perhaps you recognise yourself as one of those who have tried to hold onto a dream or passion, despite being held back by others for a long time. You may be sure if you have struggled like this that your dream is something that God has called you to do, but it seems no one is interested in it, except you. It probably seems that no one understands what you want to do, and why you want to do it. Perhaps people judge you unfairly, put you down, laugh at you or even accuse you of wrong motives. Their ridicule, discouragement or plain lack of interest can weigh you down and you may be tempted to forget your call from God.

It happened to me at one time. Most of my close friends turned away and decided they wanted nothing more to do with me. Some even said they were embarrassed to be seen talking to me. It was clear they did not want me to stand out from the crowd, to be different, or to create waves. They only wanted me to go along quietly with the group. The pain of being rejected and my isolation from friends made me want to sit down and give up, because the pain on the inside seemed unbearable. Even my wife's friends left her, and the singing group they belonged to ceased to function.

But what people did not hear was the voice of God on the inside of me, which told me never to sit down or to give up. The God I believe in helped me to carry on, and even increased my determination to do what he was calling me to do. I resolved to go forward, even at the cost of losing friends. I learned that God is my friend, one who is always there, and so I was not discouraged. Of course it was not easy, but I learned that my happiness was more complete, both when I rested on the will of God and when I pressed forward through opposition, doing what God wanted me to do.

Standing up on the inside and doing whatever you have been called to do does not mean you have to be aggressive or rude towards those who don't understand or who want to stop you. It means simply maintaining your course towards the finishing post. But dealing with the taunts of others is a skill you learn along the way. One day I was talking with someone who asked me why some people talked negatively about me. I told him, 'Let them speak what they like in the daylight, but at night they will be asleep. When they wake up, I'll be a mile away and they'll still be talking about me.' It is not necessary always to correct other people's thinking. You can just let go any hurtful or negative criticism, because time is always the greatest healer, and at the end that which is true will remain and be known.

The little boy in the story, like all children, had to obey his parent's voice, but I like to think there was the heart of a grown man in him. He understood very well that what goes on outside did not need to affect him too badly, as long as he did not bow to the pressure in his inner parts. Is this not what the blind man did when he called Jesus to his rescue while the disciples tried to silence him? He carried on calling and Jesus heard him and his vision was restored.

Having God living inside you as a Christian means that you can do even those things other people might regard as impossible. It means you can press through a crowd moving in the opposite direction. Your path to success in God's time, doing what he has ordained you to do, means you must never even think of quitting to please your mates. God has chosen you to accomplish one or more objectives in his ministry, in his time. The opposition may seem too great, but God does not call you without equipping you for the tasks ahead. Moses was given his rod with which to perform miracles. For water to be changed into wine, servants at the wedding in Cana needed appropriate jars, and they were provided. In whatever you need to achieve, God's purposes will be given at the right time.

Nobody said it was going to be an easy ride. Of course there is a temptation sometimes to sit down defeated, to quit rather than press on. God's enemy would like that and is constantly trying to stop you. It is important to admit that you cannot do it alone, because the forces of darkness getting in your way are stronger than your own ability to keep going. The only way to reach the goal is through a determination to stay in partnership with the divine powers, to be dependent on God to get you through the hardships, and to allow him to help you remain standing on the inside until you win through. It is not until you reach the finishing post that you can cry out to God, as Jesus himself did, **'I have brought you glory on earth by completing the work you gave me to do. And now, Father, glorify me in your presence.'**[49]

Hold fast and firm

I like the video of the *Lion King*. My children and I still love to watch it, even though it has been years since it was first released. There is a part when little Simba, the lion cub, is struggling not to fall off his tree as a stampede passes below him. Zazu the bird flies overhead, and shouts out, 'Hold on, Simba! Your father is coming!' That is just the encouragement you get as a Christian when times are tough, and you fear losing your grip. It is time to hold fast and firm, and not to be shaken by any passing stampede. Even when you are shaken, still keep holding, on because **'he who endures to the end shall be saved.'** (Matthew 24:13, NKJV.)

The Word of God tells us **'Christ is faithful as a son over God's house. And we are his house, if we hold on to our courage and the hope of which we boast.'**[50] There is only

49 John 17:4, 5
50 Hebrews 3:6

one thing that can turn you into a loser. If you bow to external pressure and change heart on the inside, then you will fail to do what you are called to do. Otherwise, it is the privilege of being a member of God's house that if you remain firm and faithful in the duty God has given you, then ultimately you receive a crown of glory, and walk the streets of gold. Remain confident in him, and the trouble, problem, or pressure you are facing will pass in his timing.

I encourage you to hold on to your faith, as I hold on to mine, even when it seems that everything and everyone is against you. You can remain standing firm on the inside, because you can know for yourself that Christ is the solid rock and 'all other ground is sinking sand'. When you are in Christ, and Christ in you, then you can be assured that your real life is the life within, not the circumstances you face all around you.

There is a little chorus young people like to sing: 'My God is a good God, yes, he is. My God is a good God, yes, he is. For he picks me up and turns me around, and plants my feet on higher ground. My God is a good God.' (Source unknown.) This is the Truth that can become reality for you too.

Self-confidence versus confidence in God

I came across a Bible verse a few years ago that I have leaned on ever since. It broke all the confidence I had in myself, and replaced it with confidence in God. **'For it is we who are the circumcision, we who worship by the Spirit of God, who glory in Christ Jesus, and who put no confidence in the flesh.'**[51] Whatever I do, I don't bother to worry about whether I shall be successful or not. I give it to God first in prayer and say, 'God, look at what we are just about to do. Bring glory to your name through it all.' After that, what happens next is in his hands, not mine.

God has always been against man's independent and pride-

---

51 Philippians 3:3

ful attitude. He wants him to build a sense of inward victory, which comes from the power of Christ who has promised to strengthen him. You are more than a conqueror, even before the trouble begins. The apostle Paul recognised this, and he could not prevent himself from shouting, **'Thanks be to God, who always leads us in triumphal procession in Christ and through us spreads everywhere the fragrance of the knowledge of him.'**[52]

This is the kind of confidence you can enjoy for yourself. You too can reach a stage where you are not threatened or frightened by what goes on around you. Difficulties and perplexities might come and go, but they do not bring your life to an end. Fear and anxiety, then, cannot overcome your confidence in God.

'But if not' faith

There is a Bible story of three Hebrew boys, which teaches what happens when you maintain your cool, standing up on the inside, in the face of imminent disaster. These three are perfect role models for how to keep trusting and maintaining godly principles in your life, no matter what is happening to you. The three – Shadrach, Meshach, and Abednego – were commanded by law to bow down and worship an image of gold that the cruel King Nebuchadnezzar had erected. Everyone who failed to do so was destined to end his days in the fiery furnace.

The faithful boys received a last warning, but stood up against the tyranny by saying, **'We do not need to defend ourselves before you in this matter. If we are thrown into the blazing furnace, the God we serve is able to save us from it, and he will rescue us from your hand, O king. But even if he does not, we want you to know, O king, that we will not serve your gods or worship the image of gold you have set up.'**[53]

---

52 2 Corinthians 2:14
53 Daniel 3:16-18

In God's time

This kind of faith, which we might call *'but if not'* faith, is not simple, ignorant or childlike. A decision to trust God, even if doing so would cause one to perish, is inward triumph. It dispenses with worry and casts off all fear. People who cast their cares on God, who keep trusting him, and believing that all things work together for good for those who love God, will always be successful in what they do. When you face rejection, disappointment, criticism or frustration, just keep on keeping on. At the end everything will work out according to God's will. **'Weeping may remain for a night, but rejoicing comes in the morning.'**[54]

I like the story of the man who used to worry a lot, so much in fact that his friends started to worry about him. One day, he found someone who offered to worry for him in exchange for a thousand pounds per day. Soon after the contract was signed, he met his friends, and they noticed the change in him. They became very worried that the man was not worried that day and asked him what had happened. The man joyfully explained his plan and told them how much it cost. 'A thousand pounds?' they cried. 'Where are you going to get that kind of money?'

'Ah!' replied the man calmly, 'that is the first worry he has to do for me.'

I use this funny story to illustrate a serious point. Jesus has offered to do all our worrying for us, and there is no price to pay because he has already paid it all. I know I have wasted a lot of energy from time to time, and added more problems to my life, by worrying about things instead of trusting Jesus. It is all so unnecessary, because he promises that things will work out for good anyway if only we trust him.

My dream was to start a charity to help people in my beloved Africa, and as I explained above, I was very worried when my friends deserted me. Perhaps some were jealous of

---

54 Psalm 30:5

my initiative, or thought I just wanted my own financial gain. Others might have had other reasons, known only to the heavens. I was shocked for a while, but then I realised that if I allowed them to sway me, I would fall apart inside. So I chose to trust God with my dream, and asked him to make me stand up on the inside.

Now I believe that if I do not let others rule my life, then I become a conqueror. With time I have found new, and better, friends. Clearly, anybody who wants to fly, or wants to help other people fly, is never going to have a trouble-free time. But even more importantly, I have learned that the more I give in to fear, the more fears will pursue me, and impact my life and silence me.

I found this wonderful poem some months ago. I don't know who wrote it, but my hope is that it will give you the same encouragement it gave me.

I don't understand why trials come,
But I do understand the glory when they are gone.
I don't understand when people are unkind,
But I do understand why forgiveness comes to my mind.
I don't understand when life seems unfair,
But I do understand the strength that is there.
I don't understand life's mysteries,
But I do understand your love for me.

Tempted to sit down

The story of Joseph in the Bible is a classic example of someone who was frequently tempted to sit down and keep quiet, but who refused to do so and never gave up his vision. Sold into slavery by his brothers, Joseph knew that his first task was to resist adopting a slave mentality and to learn to wait on God's timing to change his circumstances.

In God's time

Exiled in Egypt, away from family and friends, Joseph might have felt that his luck seemed always down. The rich, beautiful, and highly influential wife of Potiphar tried to seduce him. But Joseph knew this was not God's way, and it was more important to please God than to please this lovely Egyptian woman. 'How can I do such a great sin against God?' he argued to himself. Angry and hurt, Potiphar's wife had him thrown into prison. Joseph endured many years of punishment for a crime he did not commit but he still remained positive, refusing to be pulled down by the bitterness of events. Everywhere he went, Joseph made known the God he believed in and had chosen to serve. In return, in the fullness of his timing, God gave Joseph favours and exalted him far beyond anything his earthly master might have offered.

At times, God may put you through such trials. It may be that he puts you in a place where your physical body finds no comfort, or where your mind can find no rest. But it is not God's will to accommodate you; rather, he has put you where you will depend on him to achieve his mission for you. He has already prepared resources for you, so that you will be in a position to make a difference. Your only comfort and hope is in believing that wherever you are, whatever your circumstances, you can succeed.

Martin Luther once said, 'You can't keep the birds from flying over your head, but you can keep them from building a nest in your hair.' Bad times come to us all, but we do not have to believe it is a permanent state. The temptations may be inevitable, but what counts is how we deal with them. Every one of us has a choice between running away, or standing still and learning how to handle the difficult situations. **'When you are tempted, he [God] will show you a way out.'**[55]

Don't be surprised at God's provision for your way out. It isn't always what you might be expecting. God is able to use any

---

55 1 Corinthians 10:13, NLT

tool, even the devil's own work if necessary, to help you find your way forward. There was once a rat that caused a great deal of damage to a man's property. It chewed clothes and electric wires; it made holes in the man's shoes and left dirt everywhere. One day, the man cornered the rat and in its fear the rat ran headlong into the toilet bowl and was starting to drown. (You can't fall much lower than that!) The man wanted to finish it off, and reached for a broom handle to push the rat under. Quick as a flash, the rat saw the only chance of escape and grabbed the wood with a desperate bid for life, ran up the handle, jumped past the terrified man, and scuttled through the kitchen door to the safety of the bushes outside. The last thing the man saw was the rat's tail waving goodbye to him.

If you are down, feeling near to defeat or despair, start praying to see and understand the escape route that God is providing for you. While we are in our sin-restricted life, our greatest joy and the highest satisfaction are found if we work in partnership with God. There are many things we shall never understand in this life but our hopes and patience will reveal to us **'the riches of the glory of this mystery, . . . which is Christ in you, the hope of glory.'** (Colossians 1:27, KJV)

Swim your way to success

I grew up in a place in Africa where there were no rivers or lakes. The only place we could go swimming was in a reservoir constructed by local farmers for irrigation purposes. It was more of a pond, actually. It collected water from a stream overnight, and in the morning the farmers used it to water their farms. This was definitely not an Olympic pool. However, eventually when my dad, a teacher, received a job transfer, we moved to a place in the southern part of Tanzania, near Lake Malawi, into which several rivers and lakes flowed. I can vividly remember the impact of seeing so much water in one place for the first time, and how terrified I was when my new friends suggested that we should go swimming. I was about nine years old, and the fear of drowning prevented me from going into the river.

Eventually I did go in, close to the side to begin with, then a little bit deeper. One child from the village offered to help me swim out of my depth if I wanted to. She was rather older than me, perhaps thirteen or fourteen, and she was a very good swimmer by my standards. At first it went well. Then, just as she decided to let go of me, I started to flounder. I went down once, twice, then for the third time, swallowing water and feeling afraid I was going to drown. But she grabbed me, pulled me to the shore, and said with quiet confidence, 'Now you can learn to swim!' This girl helped me go where I was afraid to go. Dangerous as it was, the experience of resisting my fear built up my courage, and it took me just two weeks after the incident of near-drowning to find out what I was really capable of doing.

There's always a danger of missing out on God's blessings, and his will for our lives, because we are so used to playing it safe and walking in fear. We do those things we have always done, that others have perhaps done before, and we don't want to face any new risk. Some can argue 'Better safe than sorry!' but that does not work in God's economy. If you are one of those who fear to step out and do a new thing, be assured that when you come to the end of your life and meet with God, you will have to apologise for not doing what you were supposed to do!

Please don't misunderstand me. I am not suggesting that you leap into any old dangerous activity without thought or preparation. Don't start to do things if you are not sure God has given you permission first. On the contrary, whenever you decide to step out and do something new, you need to have made every effort to ensure that it is the voice of God you are responding to. The best way to do this is to make plenty of time for prayer before you take any action. Every time! Test it first, and then follow gently with the 'one step at a time' method. This way you gain confidence slowly that God is still anointing the activity at every step before you proceed to the next.

Your actions may seem a little bizarre to other people as you test out what you think God is telling you to do. But as long as you continue to pray, it will become clear to you if you are on the right path. Remember the story of Gideon[56] who told the men to go down to the river and drink the water. Nobody watching the scene would have understood why Gideon was

---

56 Judges 7

telling them to do that. Only God knew that this was his way of sorting the cowards from the brave fighting men who were needed for the battle, and that Gideon would be able to tell them apart by the way they drank. God's ways are not your ways, so you should be listening very carefully. If you take one step at a time, it will help you avoid the worst pitfalls that God's enemy might put in your way to prevent you from being successful. Sometimes God will take you round the obstacle by a different route. Sometimes he will ask you to wait before moving on, and that is when you will need commitment, and you will have to stand up on the inside or risk becoming discouraged.

Be prepared to admit it when you take a wrong step. Human beings are fallible, and it is silly to let pride get in your way by pretending you are always right. Better to face up to mistakes quickly, go back to prayer and wait to hear how God will re-direct you to overcome your failure and keep out of trouble.

Own your decisions

I expect, like me, you know a lot of people who ran into serious difficulties because they ended up doing what other people thought they should do. I remember a friend of mine at secondary school who always waited to hear what subjects we were swotting before deciding on his own revision plan for exams. If he had planned on doing physics, but it turned out I was tackling maths, he would put his physics book on one side and produce his maths book. If I had been busy doing matrices, he would give up on quadratic equations in order to copy me.

One of the greatest mistakes you can make is to copy some-one else, or do things that other people are pressing you to do with the goal of pleasing them. Others may have their hopes for and expectations of you, but the best solution for your life is to do the things you desire in your heart, things that are sanctioned by God. For sure, if you try to give birth to a project that you are not ordained to do, it will entail a package of problems that will be too heavy to carry.

Another course of action that is full of pitfalls is trying to draw attention to yourself. Self-styled 'celebrities' frequently end up in a sea of difficulties by trying to be people they are not; more important, more glamorous, more powerful than others. Men are often tempted by a worldly quest, but in a vain attempt to gain fame and fortune for themselves they end up trying to adopt a different personality from the one they have at home. It can't usually be sustained for long, and they experience some sort of crisis to bring them back to earth.

God honours those who stand up as themselves. He blesses those who accept responsibility for being what he has made them to be, nothing more and nothing less. Your life has a purpose, to let others know the love of God through you, and for you to know the love of God through them. The value that God puts on you does not change with your circumstances, even though you may experience one of the worst trials, for example, discrimination because of your colour, background, language ability, lack of education, or anything else. You are a child of the Most High God.

Jesus did not die for the educated, nor for those fluent in a particular language, nor for red, black, or white. He died for sinners, and from that point of view there is no first or last. We are all the same. The one who discriminates and the one who is discriminated against have both sinned and come short of the glory of God. We are all equal, and we all sail in the same boat, heading for destruction unless we remain obedient to God. There are only two groups of people in the world: those who have accepted Christ and those who have not.

There is a story from Soweto in South Africa that illustrates exactly what I mean. A priest was walking one evening through the township and came across a man lying on the ground, incapacitated by alcohol. He had soiled and wet his trousers, and seemed to have sunk to the lowest degradation possible for a human being. It pained the priest to watch, and he wondered why the man was intent on destroying his life. But as the priest stood there, he heard a soft voice whisper to him, 'The only difference between you and this man on the ground is the blood of Jesus Christ.'

As we say in the West, 'There, but for the grace of God, go I.' If you are holding this book, remember that Jesus wants you to make a difference because of your relationship with him.

Keep going to the end

One of my distant grandfathers had a very good sense of humour. He used to say, 'I can't stop eating until the spoon hits the bottom of the plate and makes a noise.' In short, he meant he couldn't stop eating till the food was all finished. The apostle Paul had a similar mindset when he said, **'I consider my life worth nothing to me, if only I may finish the race and complete the task the Lord Jesus has given me.'**[57] He urges you to finish what you start because you are never successful until you have completed what God has asked you to do. **'We have come to share in Christ if we hold firmly till the end the confidence we had at first.'**[58]

The road to success often passes the stations of hunger, cold, loneliness, prison and sometimes threats of death. Those who reach success in God's time know the secret of having quiet confidence in God while taking one step at a time. **'So do not throw away your confidence; it will be richly rewarded.'**[59] God is never a quitter. When he starts something, he will always finish it.

When we were kids, my brothers and sisters used to play

57 Acts 20:24
58 Hebrews 3:14
59 Hebrews 10:35

cards. In one of our games, an ace, a seven and a king were special, to be kept hidden till the end. As the tension mounted towards the end of the game, with everyone waiting to see who had the special cards, someone would eventually shout out, 'Game over!' and slap down the cards with a flourish. God is like that. He finishes with a big bang. So, be encouraged by the words of the apostle Paul, **'We want each of you to show the same diligence to the very end, in order to make your hope sure.'**[60]

Decide now that you do not want to become another statistic, a person who never reaches full potential. There's a Peugeot advert that says, '206 isn't just a number'. Do not be just a number where you live. Create some waves by following God's purposes. What have you got to lose? A man asked his 38-year-old wife, after sixteen years of marriage, whether she would like to go back to school and get a degree, now that the children had grown up and left home. She replied that she thought she was too old for that, and that by the time she had finished another three years in college she would be 41. The man thought about that for a second or two, and replied, 'Honey, if you don't go to college, will that make you stay 38?' The wife laughed, and took the point. Better to get older with a degree than to get older with nothing. So, too, with the wisdom of God.

From faith to faith

God will never allow your faith to remain static. He is always moving you on, helping you to grow and learn and change, and he doesn't provide all the answers for you before you set out on your journey. Zig Ziglar in his book, *See You at the Top*, says, 'Go as far as you can see, and when you reach there you will see further.' After you have climbed the first hill, you will be able to see the next peak ahead of you. And it is not just the peaks. There are many plateaus, rivers, oceans and valleys along life's journey. Each one requires a new and different step of faith, and because God is teaching you day by day, you move from faith to faith, never going backwards, always forward.

As you leave the lower ledges and forge on to higher places, there is no room for doubt or unbelief. From the first beginnings, you move every morning to new levels of faith, until you reach 'but if not' faith that tests you to the limit. Every evening you rest on new levels of confidence, in your prayers, your relationships, job, decision-making ability, and in every aspect of your life.

When I look back on things I have done, that I confidently believed God was asking me to do, I remember that in every case, almost immediately, winds would start to blow, causing me to reduce speed. I remember how my confidence used to be shaken when I met obstacles, and realise how much time and emotional energy I wasted before choosing to believe again that I was on the right track. More recently, I have had the experience of knowing that when I stand boldly and declare, 'I believe I hear from God and am led by his Spirit', then my path is clear. Boldness does not mean you become mistake-proof. But when you make a mistake, you believe that God goes ahead of you to put you on the right path again. Thinking this way helps you to do everything with peace of mind. Do not worry that you might go wrong, but use your energy to move forward and keep refining what you are doing.

When you walk with your eyes on the ground, afraid to step on the smallest insect, you won't get far quickly. So walk without fear in every area of your life. If you are afraid to take risks, it would be better to ask God to let you die, because living itself is a risky business. Men who do nothing for fear of failing inevitably fail by doing nothing. God himself is your role model and there is no better risk-taker than him. He gave his only Son,

Jesus, so that whoever believes in him should not die, but have everlasting life. He risked it all to the point of death.

If you really want to succeed in God's time, you will have to let go and swim out of your depth by trusting him, and if you do so you will find God worthy of your trust. He does not give you a dream that leads to a dead end, or impress on you ideas which terminate only in frustration. If you feel as though you are drowning, or if you are treading water out of your depth without making progress forward, then remember that God is not only the Way-maker but also the Way. He is not afraid of the deep sea because he can push back the water to let you pass on dry land. He has no concern for the depth of water because he is capable of walking on the surface. All he requires is that you put your confidence in him and follow his guidance, even when you feel lost or it looks as though you are in a dead-end place.

Chuck Swindoll says, 'If you decide you want to soar above the crowd, you will have to rise above the flatland fog that hangs over the swamp of sameness.' It is risky being different, and you will sometimes feel like you are swimming without being able to touch the bottom. But it is God's purpose to bring out the best in you, and reveal your uniqueness and special gifting, so trust him to help you learn to swim.

Be wary of those who try to manipulate you into following them. There are people who will try to make you in the mould of their own personal preferences, telling you precisely what to do, and how to do it. Some even claim they are called by God to do so, but they are self-appointed wing-clippers! Mostly what they try to achieve in the long-term is control over others, to stop their fellow men and women from growing and ultimately flying high.

The way God teaches you brings new and different blessings every day. As the scriptures say, his **'compassions never fail.**

In God's time

They are new every morning.'[61] My son, Neil is very particular about food expiry dates. He checks everything, warning us when there is something in the fridge that is close to time-up, and he refuses to eat or drink anything that is out of date. This is how God deals with us, as the story of the Hebrews in the wilderness reveals.[62] God provided his people every morning with fresh manna to eat in the desert and would not let them store any food till the following day. God never supplies you with yesterday's leftovers, but gives you the best, the freshest, the finest food every morning. He pours out his blessings on you and never asks you to go without.

To honour God, and to be the person he wants you to be, ask him in prayer for your daily bread; that means the blessings you need for the next twenty-four hours. Then ask yourself whether you are behaving like a child of God. Of course you may encounter grey days, when your cherished dream threatens to turn into a nightmare or a disaster. Sometimes your high hopes take a hike, your good intentions get lost in a comedy of errors and it really hurts. But God's blessings, coming especially through your daily reading of the scriptures, will give you the perspective you need and keep you clear headed. You can avoid doubt and despair if you follow God closely.

Take seriously God's promises to you every time minor irritations look like becoming high drama and your motivation starts slipping away. His promise to be there for you comes through like a beam of light on a foggy morning, dispelling the darkness and letting you know that all is well. God is in control when you are out of your depth. His unfailing love never ends, never wears out, never grows tired. It keeps you from total destruction. The Lord *is* wonderfully good to those who wait for him and seek him. Great *is* his faithfulness to us, and his mercies *are* fresh each morning.[62]

So, cheer up, my brother and sister. Live in the sunshine of

61 Lamentations 3:22, 23
62 Exodus 16

God's love, because you will understand it all by and by if you learn to go with his time.

Right place, right time, right attitude

Let's take a closer look at the story of Father Abraham to show how God wants us to be in a particular place, at a particular time, for his own purposes, though sometimes he reveals his reasons to us later. The Lord told Abraham, **'Go to the land I will show you.'**[63] However scary that may seem to us, we know that God is completely trustworthy, and that we have nothing to fear if he tells us to move to a new place. **'The Lord is my shepherd, I shall not be in want. . . . He makes me lie down in green pastures.'**[64] The Lord leads those who are willing to go, towards a land of his choice, not theirs.

So often we confuse our desires with God's, but when he puts us in a place, it is for his mission not ours. We can trust that ultimately it will be to our benefit and the benefit of others, though at the time we may not be able to see it. God guarantees maximum blessing and fruitfulness, and at every stage of our lives he puts us in different places and gives us different tasks and responsibilities, so that we cannot only receive his blessings at the time, but also maximise our potential for the future. To put it simply, where you are is where God wants you to be – unless you are a runner, like Jonah.

There is a great temptation to expect that the journey in life will be smooth, and hassle-free, but it is not usually so. God may tell one person simply to move house, but another may

63 Genesis 12:1
64 Psalm 23:1, 2

have to live through war or famine. Some may journey through the joy of marriage, and others may have to endure severe pain or disability. But understanding that we are where we are because God has put us there helps us to trust, and removes our fears and doubts. From that point we have confidence to do what God wants us to do, not just to follow our own desires.

The Bible story of Joseph is one of the best examples to illustrate this. Here was a young man, sold into slavery by his own blood brothers, yet rising to the highest position in the Egyptian government under Pharaoh. Joseph was unaware of his destiny, and the route to the palace took him to the lowest levels, physically, spiritually and emotionally. He was thrown into a pit by his brothers, sold as a slave, and then suffered the shame of being falsely accused as a rapist and humiliated in prison while knowing his innocence. Not just one pit, but, as the popular expression goes, he went through the pits!

'When Joseph came to his brothers, they stripped him of his robe – the richly ornamented robe he was wearing – and they took him and threw him into the cistern [pit]. Now the cistern was empty; there was no water in it.'[65] The whole point of a pit is to trap so that no escape is possible. It is a dark and terrifying place to be. I remember seeing a pit on one of our farms when I was growing up, and asked my dad what it was for. He told me pits were dug in the path of wild pigs, to stop them from destroying the crops. Once a pig had fallen into a pit, it would never come out alive. A pit is a place of destruction, and Joseph's brothers planned to use it to destroy him. But, as it is for him who trusts in God and believes that he is where God has placed him, God was in the pit with Joseph and indeed all the way on his long walk to the Egyptian palace. He believed that God was the only One who could get him out and help him succeed, and so he did not give way to

65 Genesis 37:23, 24

fears that he was in the wrong place. Rather the opposite. He remained positive that God would keep him on track to his destiny. And so it is with all of us. God has a palace position ready for us, but we may get there only through very difficult circumstances, and take a route we were not expecting.

Getting to the palace

Have you ever tried to get a job in a palace? It is no easy task. For a start, you have to be the right nationality and pass all kinds of security checks, because of the ease of access to important people and documents. Joseph wasn't the right nationality at all. As a Hebrew slave in Egyptian territory he would have had no chance of getting work at the palace, except that his life was in God's hands. He had the qualities that God was looking for, and was willing to trust him for the journey.

This applies to you, too. God weighs and matches your qualities and your abilities to the level of difficulty you may have to pass through on your way to the palace. He grants you the staying power to cope and survive trying situations en route. If you let God lead, you will be in 'green pastures', but if you run, hide, or disobey, like Adam and Eve, or Jonah, you find yourself in places God did not put you.

Having the right attitude

It is not enough to be in the palace, either. It is also important to have the right attitude once you arrive, and this means making a simple choice: whether you are going to look down or up. Do you want to see mud? Or stars? Your attitude is determined by whether you want to look at the darkness, see the worst in every situation, and get depressed, or whether you look up towards the light, have hope and consider every situation as a potential springboard in God's hands. This is not a trivial matter. Even if you have been given the opportunity of starting the journey in the palace, if your attitude is bad you will most likely end up in the pit.

The Bible story of Haman and Mordecai from the Book of Esther may demonstrate the point. Haman had an important role next to the king, but his heart was full of hunger for power, manipulative plans, and hatred of the Jews, and his attitude brought his life to an end by his being hanged on the gallows prepared for Mordecai. It is not only being in the right place or right position that makes you successful, but also what flows out of your heart, which speaks of your success or failure.

The point is also revealed in the life of the late Princess Margaret, younger sister to Queen Elizabeth II. Born into the royal family, grew up in a palace, respected as a royal princess, enjoyed all the privileges of being the daughter of a king, and later the sister of the Queen, but ended her life sadly. Perhaps you might say in the pits. This is what the *Daily Express* wrote about her the morning after her death:

Princess Margaret was transformed from royal beauty to a frustrated and pitiful figure. The final years in the life of the Queen's sister were turned into a nightmare. . . . Within the space of a decade she was transformed from a dazzling and vivacious princess to a pale shadow of her former self.[66]

It is not the palace that transforms you; it is what you do in the palace that will make you succeed or fail in your life. Many sons and daughters of kings and queens start off with the finest opportunities and enough privileges to soar above any clouds of misfortune, but misuse their lives with wrong attitudes and end up doing nothing to help themselves or others. Another modern-day example is Osama bin Laden, a royal descendant with attitude problems. He has become a fugitive, hunted like a wild dog because of his wrong choices. Biblical examples include Absalom, the son of King David, and King Belshazzar of Babylon.

---

66 *Daily Express*, 11 February 2002

In God's time

If you are honest with yourself, you will see that your journey through life is not so very different from that of one of royal descent. You are the child of a king, the King of the Universe. The attitude you have today is important, because it will determine where you end up, either in the palace where you belong, or in the pits. There are only two destinations: The choice is yours.

Many people wear T-shirts, badges, or caps sporting words like 'I love Jesus', or 'Jesus saves'. However, the badge of Christianity is not something for the outside. Rather, it is a sign revealing the union and fellowship between God and man. The world will be convinced that God sent his Son as its Redeemer only when there is seen in the followers of Christ the power of grace, manifested in the transformation of character.

This is the real reason for Joseph's ultimate success. Despite his humiliation in being falsely convicted of rape, what the Egyptians finally saw in him was the power of God's grace in his attitude. If we Christians are going to win the argument in favour of the Gospel, we have to be loving and lovable people. The world should be able to see the love of God not only in the creation of the natural world, but also in us and the way we handle the situations we are thrown into. We could say that our attitude determines our altitude!

Moses was an outrageous man, slow of speech, distrustful and with low self-esteem, but he had the right attitude to God's direction for his life and he did not refuse to go where God wanted him to go. As he submitted to God, Moses' character slowly changed, and he became polite, eloquent, self-possessed and fitted for the greatest mission ever entrusted to a human being. The Bible writes of Moses, **'Since then, no prophet has risen in Israel like Moses, whom the Lord knew face to face.'**[67]

Moses is a good role model for us. By accepting the

---

67 Deuteronomy 34:10

duty that God puts on us, we show that we love him, and are totally dependent on him. Any job we receive from God will require an exercise of will, and God blesses our readiness to serve him in obedience. If we feel in any way that our work is not valued or appreciated, but we still believe that God wants us for some higher calling, we should bear in mind that only God has the power to put us where we fit. **'He brings one down, he exalts another.'**[68]

Every one of us has a recognised place in the everlasting plan of God. Our success depends on how willing we are in our faithfulness and co-operation with God. Our attitude should be, 'I am treated and placed in a better position than Jesus was.' We should remind ourselves that the Son of Man did not even have a place to put his head. Jesus owned no house, no car, not even a small plot of land.

When you think about your attitude, remember as well that God does not keep a place for those who delight more in winning a crown than in carrying the cross. He is looking for people who are going to get on with the work rather than worry about what their reward might be at the end. So your task should be to refine your attitude, and to be conscientious in doing good work, not to think about fame or promotion along the way.

The Bible story of the crippled man who lay waiting near the pool for thirty-eight years shows the power of attitude. When Jesus asked him if he wanted to be healed, he said, **'Sir, . . . I have no-one to help me into the pool when the water is stirred.'** And he added, **'While I am trying to get in, someone else goes down ahead of me.'**[69] Jesus ordered him, **'Get up! Pick up your mat and walk.'**

Maybe you, too, have some physical condition that you feel prevents you from living normally. It is important not to let your circumstances steal your initiative. Do you have a negative atti-

68 Psalm 75:7
69 John 5:1-8

tude, or do you lack confidence because of living in a horrible place, or because of something that happened to you in the past? Maybe your marriage failed. Maybe you did not get the chance of a good education. Stand up, and do not feel sorry for yourself over what happened. Jesus understands that being full of self-pity will not help your condition, so he orders you like the lame man to get up, to pick up your problems and walk!

There is no point at all in sitting around complaining, blaming others, or pitying yourself. Your attitude determines everything, so accept the freedom from Jesus, be strong, powerful and move on. Stop asking the 'why me?' question because it reveals an attitude of a defeatist. It puts a chip on your shoulder and you can't stand tall.

If you are tempted to compare yourself with others, then start comparing yourself with those who are less fortunate than you. Don't say, like the man in the story, that someone else always goes first. You also can go first. If you only have one eye, then compare yourself to those who are blind. And if you insist on looking at those who are in better positions, then do so in order to catch something of a vision, and imagine where you may be, eventually, if you co-operate with God. Remember that God is not a respecter of persons. He gives rain and sunshine equally to those who are in the same place, and twenty-four hours in every day to all alike.

Shake well before use

We have said how important it is to hold correct beliefs about the situations we find ourselves in, so that we maintain a right attitude, even in difficult circumstances. Most societies have allowed some of their beliefs to come from superstitions about animals, instead of from God. In England it is supposed to be 'lucky' to pass a black cat, and where I come from people become suspicious if an owl lands on their foot at night and starts hooting. In the Zimbabwean film entitled *Neria* the scene opens with a snake slithering in front of a man on a bicycle, and everyone immediately understands that this is a bad omen.

So it was in biblical times. **'When Paul had gathered a bundle of sticks and laid them on the fire, a viper came out because of the heat, and fastened on his hand. So when the natives saw the creature hanging from his hand, they said to one another, "No doubt this man is a murderer, whom, though he has escaped from the sea, yet justice does not allow to live." But he shook off the creature into the fire and suffered no harm.'[70]**

Everybody made an instant judgement on Paul on the basis of this bad omen, and Paul might have thought God had finally given up on him. Not only had he been shipwrecked to within an inch of his life, but was then bitten by a poisonous snake and taken to be a murderer as well. Everyone present that day believed the apostle Paul had only a few hours to live, seeing the snake wrapped around his arm like that. But no one saw the faith in his heart. The verses do not say that he jumped back in horror, or that he screamed out in fear. Instead, he shook off the creature into the fire and suffered no harmful effects.

You, too, may be wrapped up by Satan, to an extent that everyone around believes you will never get out. But nothing is impossible for the Lord, and your success will be determined by your attitude, and your faith in God to pull you free. Do not let the snakebites of the past become an obstacle to the bright dreams for your future. Like Paul, you can shake off the spirit of coldness and deadness inside you, and go to war against the fear of snakes around you.

Jesus is eagerly waiting to make you whole – physically, financially, morally, spiritually, mentally and emotionally – and

70 Acts 28:3-5, NKJV

In God's time

he is ready with his spanners to give you an overhaul. But remember, he does not offer any quick fixes. His plan offers you everlasting life, and he gives you free and full insurance cover. Your only responsibility is to say 'Yes', no matter what snakes may be threatening at the time.

Jesus' mission on earth is for you to have life, and life more abundantly. If you think you have certain weaknesses and can't move forward, then ask him and he will move you. If you believe you have committed so many sins, he will tell you that his grace is sufficient. If you claim that you failed yesterday, he will reassure you that he is faithful and just to forgive.

I am sure you have come across liquid medicine or other products displaying the label 'Shake Well Before Use'. That is good advice for us. Shake yourself well, and shake off negative attitudes and wrong beliefs about God because they hold you back. Stand up like a man or woman of God, and make a decision to follow him one step at a time. If you do so, **'He will lift you up and make your lives significant.'**[71] If you have read it, take it in and believe it. Have confidence that you will be lifted up, and that you will be made whole and significant.

---

71 James 4:10, Amplified Bible

Dream your way to success

As a young boy, before he went through his uncomfortable journey towards the palace, our friend Joseph was a dreamer. That is what his brothers called him when they saw him coming. 'Here comes the dreamer,' they said to one another. Joseph had big plans to improve things for his family, and his nation, and he had even bigger plans for God. No wonder he was a target for Satan, who wants us all sitting around doing nothing. Perhaps we should be listening to Joseph's example. Dreaming about doing something great for God right where we are is a possible challenge available to all of us. Can you dream of making an impact on events in some way for your community, for your country, for your church, and for your family? Your dream can start right here.

Maybe you feel you cannot perform well because you have been placed in a bad position to start with. However, when God draws up the athletes for the race, he does not start them in a straight row, like in the 100m sprint. No, he staggers the line-up so that the runners all start from different positions, like in the 200m sprint. I have never heard of a champion complaining about his starting position and using it as an excuse to fail. No matter where you are positioned to start with, you can have a big finish as a champion if you allow God to pour his blessings on your dream right there. Your desert will spring water.

There are two examples from the Bible to illustrate the point. Firstly, let's look at what happened to Abraham and his nephew Lot. Abraham gave the choice of starting place away, and ended up being blessed beyond his dreams.[72] Meanwhile, Lot tried to choose what he thought was the more advantageous starting place for himself and his wealth, but he ended up losing his family, and committed adultery with his two young daughters.[73]

Secondly, there is the example of Daniel. What could be a worse pit than a den of lions? Yet Daniel was spared because of his faith, and those who wanted him dead were not only eaten by the lions themselves, but their wives and children too.[74]

So, having accepted that you are where God has put you, and that this is the starting place for your vision of success, move on and be specific about what you want to achieve. If you allow vagueness to creep in, you may not generate enough confidence to take off. Like an eagle preparing to fly, you need to flap the wings a little, to get enough energy for lift-off. Then you will be able to soar above the clouds and high into the sky.

Go for straight talking. Be open, bold and straightforward about your dream. Have confidence, and remember that the way you come across to others is even more important than what you say. If your heart is filled with truth, honesty, holiness and love, then you will automatically have a positive influence on others.

Wear the right garments for your dream

Everyone understands the need for a dress code. What you wear has to be appropriate for the job, so that people can recognise who you are and take you seriously. Few of us would be comfortable with the treatment in hospital if the nurse

72 Genesis 13:9-13
73 Genesis 19:23-38
74 Daniel 6:16-24

showed up wearing an army uniform, and equipped with rifles or pistols. I once saw a white man in Tanzania wearing his smart British winter jacket – I don't suppose he got much work done!

As Christians, we also have a dress code, but it consists more of inside character than outside clothing, and it is revealed in the way we act. Nevertheless, we can put it on like a garment. Indeed, the scriptures command us to 'Put on love'.

Jesus calls us to lead a better and greater life, full of energy and power, but we have first to take off the old garment of deadness. This is what happened when Jesus raised his friend Lazarus from the dead. **'Jesus called in a loud voice, "Lazarus, come out!" The dead man came out, his hands and feet wrapped with strips of linen, and a cloth around his face. Jesus said to them, "Take off the grave clothes and let him go."'**[75]

When you fail to take off your grave clothes, you prohibit yourself from receiving the new life of fullness. So be firm in your decision to follow Christ. Set your mind to it, and hear Jesus calling, 'Come out!' To get out of the pit and start moving to the palace, you not only have to accept the position; you also have to wear the new garment. You cannot enter the palace dressed in your old grave clothes.

Your character is the garment you choose to wear according to the work you are doing. To pursue your dream, you need to exchange the old for the new one from Jesus and, as the scriptures command, 'put on love'[76]. This means loving and trusting God who is faithful, not human beings who will most often let you down.

I recently came across a sad newspaper article from Tanzania, over the Internet. It told of a twenty-year old girl who died on the way to hospital having swallowed twenty malaria tablets. She left a pitiful note to her aunt, explaining that she

75 John 11:43-44
76 Colossian 3:14

had decided to end her life because her boyfriend had gone away to marry someone else.

Your life is your own, and if you decide to end it, no one else can give it back to you. When you put your hopes in human beings, they will disappoint you some day, and it will seem as if there is nothing left to live for. God does not treat you this way. He may put you through trials, but he does not desert you. Rather the opposite: he seeks to establish you strongly and safely. Marry yourself to Jesus, and you will never be so disappointed that you are tempted to take your own life.

In the Scriptures there is a story that helps to explain the dangers you face if you do not exchange your old grave clothes for the new garment of life from Jesus. A king prepared a wedding feast for his son, and invited not only his friends but also the wealthy people in his town. The day of the wedding came, and not one of the invited guests turned up. The king was very unhappy, and so he ordered his servants to invite everyone they met in the streets. The servants did so, and there was a huge wedding feast. The food was yummy, and the drinks were flowing, and everyone was having a good time. Later, the king came to see his guests, and in the crowd he spotted someone wearing old clothes. The man was speechless when the king asked him how he had got in without wedding clothes. The servants were ordered to tie the man's arms and legs and throw him out into the darkness.[77]

Dream your dreams of success, but be sure your clothes do not accuse you and prohibit you from achieving that success. The safest garment is the one you receive from Jesus Christ. It is the armour of light, which will enable you to overcome the evil one.

Turning your dream into success requires patience, and practice, and we are going to look at several different aspects of

---

77 Matthew 22:1-14

this. Let me introduce you to the vital ingredients right here, and then expand in greater detail over the next few chapters.

Work steadily towards your dream

Your dream cannot be built upon a foundation of luck, or wishful thinking. Wherever God has put you, he has prepared resources for you to use, and there is no time to wait around for things just to happen. First among the resources you have been given is your own creative power to make things happen. You may occasionally find some small success without much effort, but more usually you will have to work through waves and storms before reaching what you dreamed of. You will often be taken beyond your comfort zone.

God blesses what you do, not what you plan or how you feel. Even those who trust to luck, like those who play the lottery or gamble in casinos, have to do something for success, either buy a ticket, or place their bets at the table. And the principle is all the more true for Christians, who have rejected the idea of luck. First you have to pray, and then you have to work. The effort you put into prayer allows God to enable and favour you, while work releases your own creative power and energy. When God's favour is mixed with human work, it creates an unstoppable force. It is important to understand that prayer can never be a substitute for effort. If you want to see fruit, first you have to till the soil and plant your garden with the seeds of your choice, but then draw water from the ground.

Your ability to create something from the work you do comes from creative power God put into you, which nobody can ever take away, except your own decision not to use it. Drawing from such a natural resource is as simple as trees drawing water from the ground. In fact, God has likened us to a tree planted by a river[78]. Feeding on the goodness placed inside you determines what you are like on the outside.

---

78 Psalm 1:3

Pray faithfully for your dream

Prayer is not a substitute for work, nor can we get away with thinking it is unimportant. Your time in prayer with God is essential, and has many purposes: it sets your priorities right when you pray before acting; it will open paths ahead of you which you may not have been expecting; it will help you keep alive your vision or dream, and give you the drive and determination to pursue it; and, above all, it will enable you to act the right way in difficult circumstances. I always like to remind myself that there is nothing good that God and I cannot do, regardless of how difficult it might be, so long as God is directing me.

If you are not sure that you understand what God wants you to do, then ask in prayer. **'Ask God, because he gives to all liberally and without reproach, and it will be given to you.'**[79] Then take the time to listen very carefully. Sometimes we miss what God is saying, because we think the answers are to be found outside us, like a loud voice calling out from the sky. But you are fearfully and wonderfully made, and God has put his still small voice of creativity in your heart. You already have within you many of the answers to the questions you always ask, so be wise and listen to his voice from within you. Other answers can be found in creation, which reveals the divine nature, and still others can be found through our fellow human beings. There are few questions that concern us that God has not already answered.

Prayer is not just about asking questions. It is the greatest delight of God, our Father, to see human beings accept the gifts and powers he has put in them, so that they can accomplish their divine roles and purposes. He wants all of them, wherever they have been placed, to achieve greatness, and when they pray, God conveys his blessing to them and in return they can give him their thanks.

79 See James 1:5

Share your dream

Sharing your life and your vision with others is also a way in which both you and other people can receive blessings from God, and gain encouragement, because people produce better results when they work together. It can be likened to cross pollination in the fruit garden from which both trees benefit. Don't be afraid to draw from the experience of others, because it is not stealing, more like sharing pollen. It is not possible to steal all of someone else's pollen. You, too, can give generously of your time and talents to benefit others and encourage them on their way.

Those who possess more creative power than you can strengthen you, and there is no need to feel threatened by competition. You are not diminished just because someone else has more. The bluebells flourish in the shade of big trees, but they are no less beautiful, and even a huge tree standing in the middle of fertile land may need another to cross-pollinate it before it is able to bear fruit. We are all dependent on one another to help each one grow; and our sharing of ideas, gifts and time, in a partnership of encouragement, is as essential to us as the sharing of sunlight, water, and deep rich soil is to the trees and flowers.

Of course, you will meet those who do not think this way, those who are unwilling to bless others as they go, and you will need to be discerning as you search for people you can cross-pollinate with. Some are like parasites, who want to drink from you, to draw from your life, but who contribute nothing to your vision and dream. Such folk are likely to drain you to death. But you can choose to draw close to those who have a similar ambition to yours, who want to grow and be creative like you. Look around you and select as friends and colleagues people who want to edify one another and become more productive.

In God's time

Revise your dream

Your dream is not a static block of concrete, but something that will grow and change with you, if you let it. As God's plan for you unfolds day by day, he puts you in different places to challenge and refine you and make you develop. Even though you may feel fearful because you don't know what may happen tomorrow, take the time to focus on your life goals. Revise and revise again to master your mission, and master the art of listening to God's voice. He moves you on in the right direction, so do not linger too long in one place. If you find yourself stuck, then question whether you have ended up in a dead end or cul-de-sac that takes you nowhere. Go back to the map and be observant of the landmarks.

Through it all, hear the voice of God who encourages you all the time. He will show you **'the goodness of the Lord in the land of the living. Wait on the Lord; be of good courage, and He shall strengthen your heart; wait, I say, on the Lord!'**[80]

---

80 Psalm 27:13-14, NKJV

The right company

'**U**nless the Lord builds the house, its builders labour in vain.'[81] God, in his time, has placed us where we can receive all the benefits of salvation, as long as we are prepared to ask for them. Our success in the world depends on the extent to which we submit ourselves to God's plan, which he prepared for us even before our parents brought us into the world. **'All the days ordained for me were written in your book before one of them came to be.'**[82]

The first contact we make with other people as we come into this world through birth is with our families. Mum and Dad form our first station in the journey of life, then our siblings and other close relatives, and normally they are supportive, though there are some exceptions. Eventually we grow up, move out and make our own friends and neighbours. And throughout the whole of our lives we shall need all kinds of support from others; moral support, emotional and spiritual support, physical and financial support. 'No man is an island,' said the poet John Donne, and I agree.

To achieve the support we need, we tend to gravitate towards those we feel have things in common with us, and form bonds around being together and doing things together for pleasure. We pick our company very often according to whether or not we think others have sympathy with our way of

81 Psalm 127:1
82 Psalm 139:16

looking at the world, and the values we hold dear. These, in turn, have been forged from a combination of personality, habits, beliefs, education and the choices we have made in the past, until ultimately our inward character is revealed in our outward behaviour.

But in any relationship, whether consciously or unconsciously, there is a process of mutual influence going on. The values we hold and the behaviour we display day to day motivate others to accept or reject our company, and dictate whether we live in harmony or conflict with the people around us. The same values will play a major role in our decision-making processes, and the final choices we make. Without any particular effort on our part, they inevitably impact on our families, our communities, and ultimately our national characteristics. In a broader sense we call them culture.

Sadly, we live in a world of 'Monkey see, monkey do', and so very often the way we behave as adults is a repetition of all that we saw adults do when we were growing up. There is a tendency for most of us to want to fit in. After watching others, we copy their behaviour even if it changes us for the worse. Jesus gave us cautionary words about this, as he watched the spiritual leaders of his day (the Pharisees) going about their daily routines. He said, **'Do not do what they do, for they do not practise what they preach.'**[83] In other words, the lesson he was teaching was that the way we behave is far more important than any fine words we might be speaking.

All this is food for thought when we are choosing the right company. If those we associate with on a daily basis do not walk the way they talk, then there is a question mark on their integrity, and we need to be alert. It also helps us to understand why it is of paramount importance that we present healthy role models of behaviour to our children, and make sure they have the opportunity to imitate good conduct when they grow up.

83 Matthew 23:3

Parents

In the story of the prodigal son (Luke 15), when the young man asked for his inheritance and walked away from his father, you might wonder what drew him back home again. It is clear from the story that the father was full of love and understanding, so it is likely that the boy cherished memories of the good times he had had with his father before he left home. He battled in his mind for quite a good while, asking himself how long he should stay in a dead-end place, feeding the pigs and wishing he had enough food for his own stomach. He pictured the servants back home, eating their fill, and filling the bins with leftovers. I think he even remembered how well the dogs used to eat, and compared that to his present state of hunger and misery. Truly, good memories of our early families draw us back to our parents, and keep us on the right track in adult life. The Bible says, **'Train a child in the way he should go, and when he is old he will not turn from it.'**[84]

As one of twelve children, I can't understand how my mum and dad managed to cope with the pressure of bringing us all up. My mother, who died last year at the age of eighty-one, must have had very good nerves, because all of us have happy memories of our childhood. When we meet at home, we sometimes talk and laugh the whole night. My dad had a very special way of celebrating our return home during the holidays. He used to give us a goat or a lamb from his farm to eat as a meal, and we would barbecue it on an open fire, and talk and tell jokes all through the night. Even now, though my parents are no longer there, fond memories of the place where I grew up compel me to go back sometimes, and re-experience the feeling of belonging there. Home sweet home.

Future behaviour and attitudes are formed through a positive relationship with parents during childhood. The home should

84 Proverbs 22:6

therefore be a place where youngsters will be developed in all their capabilities and talents, and where their spiritual gifts will be nurtured, so that they have the energy to go through life with excellence. You cannot choose your parents, but you can choose how to be one. If you bless your children with your actions as well as your words, and if you bring them up according to God's plan, you will affirm them as God's workers who need not be ashamed of their calling.

Do not be like the spiritual leaders of Jesus' day, who said the right things but acted badly. Mahatma Ghandi once said, 'If Christians were like Christ, I would be one too.' Unfortunately, the ones he met preached about love, but practised discrimination. They talked about sharing, but they practised selfishness. When it comes to exercising influence as parents, we have to practise what we preach, and devote time and energy to creating happy memories for our children. Like father like son, they say. If you are privileged to have children, try to observe them, and most likely you will see yourself in them in some of their activities or behaviours. Give them a good example and a good foundation for their character. Introduce them to the One who loves them, and died for them, and they will never leave him, even when they are old.

Friends

We can't choose our parents but can at least choose our friends. The company of people you hang around with will affect how long it takes for you to reach the roof of success, and choosing wrongly can seriously threaten your goals. Good friends will support you, and help to keep you away from trouble. The choice you make as to the company you keep, your relationships with God, family and community, will be affected one way or another. Remember, when you wear gloves to go and work in muddy soil, it is the glove that gets dirty, not the soil that gets 'glovy'. Have this in mind as you read on.

One of the best ways to get things moving in your life is to come alongside others who are achievers. You can watch how they work, learn how they think and put what you learn into practice in your own life. It is a sure recipe for success. Read books by those who have achieved in the field you are interested in. Listen to tapes, and watch videos by others with expertise. You will become like the people you spend time with, so choose to be among those who can draw you to success.

Here is a delightful story from the natural world to encourage you when it comes to picking friends. Pelicans along the beach at Monterey in California used to feed on fish discarded by fishermen. They got so accustomed to free meals that they forgot their natural ability to dive and catch fish. After a while, environmentalists protested and the fishing activities were stopped. However, with their easy meals gone, some of the pelicans were starving to death. The environmentalists came to their rescue by bringing in pelicans from another area, to help retrain the spoiled birds. The newly-introduced birds went fishing each day, and it was not long before the starving birds started to copy their survival techniques. They learned to fish for themselves again.

Picking friends from among those who can help and support us is a vital step towards becoming successful. We should not associate with people who do not share our ambitions and goals for life. The Bible says, **'Bad company corrupts good character.'**[85] When the Israelites were approaching the Promised Land, God instructed them to drive out the inhabitants of the land, because **'those you allow to remain will become barbs in your eyes and thorns in your sides. They will give you trouble.'**[86] God was not being uncharitable! Rather, he was protecting the Israelites from being corrupted by a people who had no knowledge of God.

85 1 Corinthians 15:33
86 Numbers 33:55

In God's time

God understood that the Israelites had been wounded in Egypt and in their journey through the desert. They were weak and vulnerable, and their minds had not yet fully grasped God's love and his ways. There was a real danger that if God let his precious children associate with the Canaanites they would pick up their habits and values, seek their approval, model their behaviour, and end up worshipping their gods. The Israelites might all too easily forget the life mission and purpose that God had planned for them.

Many young people claim that they know what they are doing when they hang out with friends of questionable characters. They do not believe bad relationships will hurt them, and may even believe they are able to influence their chosen friends for good. But young people have unformed minds and spirits that have never been tested. They are vulnerable, like the Israelites, and need protection. Many young lives are damaged or ruined by corruption after joining a group of friends who pull them down. A toxic relationship works like a cancer cell, destroying all the healthy cells around it. Unless it is cut out, it can ruin your health and lead to death.

Sociologists, and those who study the effects of human behaviour on others, say that if you live to be seventy years old, you may influence up to 10,000 people for better or worse, whether you know you are doing so or not. John Maxwell says that 'you will acquire the vices and virtues of your closest associates. The fragrance of their lives will pervade yours.'

When I was about fourteen years old I read a quotation from Cervantes, the writer of *Don Quixote*. 'Tell me your company and I will tell you who you are.' Your friends will both mould and motivate you, and you will begin to change to be like them. If you are mature and strong you may be able to influence people positively, but as you are still forming your vision and learning the ways of God, then avoid bad company.

Remember that their constant dripping will wear away a stone, and their characters and habits can undermine you little by little, and day by day. Choose your support team carefully, and benefit from the blessings.

Your career

Your choice of career is going to be one of the most important decisions in your life, simply because you spend so much time at work – eight to ten hours a day and five days a week on average. For that reason alone you need to be listening to God's guidance from within to help you choose. It is counter-productive to work at something just to please other people, parents or teachers, for example, or to pursue a career to impress people. When you do so, you live a life of lies, lose respect for yourself and suffer depression and isolation.

God has given you the ability to choose the career that is best for you, and it is far more important to follow the anointing of God than to live in fear of upsetting the feelings of parents or friends. Your chosen work should bring you spiritual well being, and not be in conflict with your Christian values and ethics. This is also true if you start up your own business and have to make ethical judgements about the way to run it. To be at peace with yourself, and to journey steadily towards your goal, you cannot choose work that undermines you spiritually, or distracts you from God's purposes.

Moses, you will recall, was found in the bulrushes and brought up by an Egyptian princess, the daughter of the Pharaoh, and he would have gone on thinking of himself as an Egyptian had it not been for God's call upon his life. Recognising his true identity, he refused to be called 'the son of Pharaoh's daughter', and went on to become the leader of the Israelites out of Egypt to the Promised Land.

Whether you are an employer or an employee, you can learn

to control your life and maximise your potential. Learn to say 'yes' or 'no' at work at the right time and to the right person. This can be particularly hard for those who were taught always to please their parents, teachers, priests and other authority figures. Many people are brought up to say what others want to hear, and to avoid criticism and conflict. But you are master of your own destiny, and as you grow in your vision for the future you can learn to take the right stuff for your journey and deal with conflict in a more adult way. The most successful people know when to say 'yes' or 'no', even to those they love.

A quick look at the lives of King Herod and Pontius Pilate, for example, will show you what happens when people find it hard to say 'no' The most innocent people in the history of the world, Jesus Christ and his cousin John the Baptist, were killed precisely because these two courted popularity, and gave the answers others wanted to hear. As he did with Moses, and dozens of other characters in the Bible stories, God has prepared work for you to do. Learn to take an inventory of your working life every day, and check that you are sticking to God's plan for you.

Your spouse

Choosing your partner for life requires the utmost care and testing before God. When you become one with your partner, you inevitably open yourself to the spirit that is at work within that person. So, look for someone who shares your values, and whose character is in harmony with your own Christian character. Don't kid yourself that you will be able to change someone's character through marriage. You need someone who can challenge you to reach your highest potential, and understand life from the divine perspective. The best partner is someone who can speak God's word into your life, because it comes from his or her heart, not because he or she has learned it parrot fashion. The blessings will flow if you choose a partner who can give you a double portion of the spirit of God.

When you think about spending a lifetime with someone, remember that your company will influence your conduct, and your conduct will shape your character. Ultimately, your character will shape your destiny without your even noticing. There is a strong tendency to become like the people you spend most time with. A well-known proverb says that **'a man is known by the company he keeps.'**[87] If this is true of friends, how much more true is it of a spouse with whom you spend even more time?

Trust your partner sufficiently to disclose your real self without fear, especially in those areas where you feel inadequate or vulnerable, and encourage your partner to do the same. From this position of mutual weakness and vulnerability you will be able to offer mutual prayer, support and encouragement. Watch the language you use and the actions you take: hurtful remarks, unspoken compliments, good intentions postponed and un-offered gifts, all contribute to a poor relationship. So continue day by day to love your spouse, and learn to appreciate the other as a gift. No one can do this for you. God said, **'and they will become one flesh'**,[88] meaning that the way you treat your partner will rebound on you too. The way you treat your body should be the way you treat your wife. Love your wife as Christ loved the church; die for her if you have to.

Make an agreement with your partner that you will give each other full support in all your activities, so that whatever your success you can enjoy it together. Your achievements will count for little if they end up causing rivalry, arguments, or a bitter split between the two of you in court. It is important to remember, as well, that no relationship can thrive if there is no investment of time and effort in it. Even though he was a great Christian leader, Nelson Mandela's marriage to Winnie sadly foundered,

87 See also Proverbs 27:19
88 Genesis 2:24

to his heart-felt disappointment, because his enforced separation from her through imprisonment prevented him from investing enough time in building the relationship. Despite the hope and anticipation of reunion after twenty-seven years of being apart, these two were unable to enjoy together the benefits of their beliefs for which they had so courageously fought. Investment in your marriage is an investment towards your own success, as well as that of your partner's, and sacrificial investment reaps the highest benefits.

Spend time together because, as it stands, TIME is Treasure Invested in Man while on Earth. Spend this treasure to enrich each other. If God invested his time in making you, you can as well invest your time in building and developing your spouse.

Pray your way to success

As already outlined in Chapter 9, prayer is one of the most important ingredients in making a successful life, and so it should be at the very centre of all our activities. There is no greater force to be reckoned with in this world than a man or woman who prays. There is no higher human hope than that of being linked and united with heaven, so that we can tap the Creator's power in our lives and the lives of those we love. The key is to find out how prayer works, and to get rid of any illusions you may have about it, because sooner or later they will cause you to give up praying. From that springboard, you can learn when and how to pray, exactly what to pray for, and how to structure your prayer life. Anyone aspiring to succeed in life should press on to experience the supernatural powers that God has available for him. It is our prayer life that testifies more clearly than anything else to our belief in God and to our relationship with him as a Father.

Joyce Mayer says, 'Every failure is in essence a prayer failure.'[89] If you fail to pray, you invite failure itself into your life and block the road to success. Prayer is a key that unlocks the stores of heaven for God to move on our behalf, and bring the change we so greatly desire into our lives.

Perhaps you have tried to pray but found it difficult, or perhaps you started to pray well, and gradually tailed off to the

89 Joyce Mayer, *How to Succeed at Being Yourself*

In God's time

point where you became dissatisfied with your prayer life. I have been in that place too, and many Christians today share similar frustrations, often feeling that their prayers are not good enough, or strong enough, or not quite right in one way or another. Take heart! The disciples of Jesus' day had the same problems, and they asked Jesus to teach them how to pray. Even the apostle Paul went through the same kind of trouble, until he finally understood that the Holy Spirit helped him in prayer, and that Jesus was always there to intercede for everyone who tries to pray. This is the encouragement you need, too. If both Jesus and the Holy Spirit are working away in prayer for you, then you can be assured that God the Father hears.

In addition to this, there are some easy guidelines to understanding what makes prayer effective which you can follow. Understanding the way in which God acts in the world, and the partnership the Father wants to create with his people will help you to persevere when prayer gets difficult.

How prayer works

Prayer, and its effects, is a divine science that human beings can hardly comprehend. It is very difficult to explain how it works because we are not givers but recipients of the results of our prayers. The only way we can even begin to know how prayer works is to pray. Even when we pray, we will not necessarily know how it works, but it *will* change our lives. So we must just say our words, addressing them to God through the name of Jesus, and the rest is the result and fulfilment of God's promise: 'Call me and I will deliver you and I will show you great things you have never seen.' Jesus said, 'Ask and it will be given to you.' Prayer works only if we pray. Simple.

Partnership with God

When the Creator made human beings he gave them a free

choice, whether to do good or evil, and he has not changed his mind since. We still have to exercise our free will today, whether to walk in the light following the path offered by Jesus, or go our own way. God has agreed to act in the world to bring about good only if we ask him to. Otherwise, what happens is the result of our own ideas, plans and effort. So, prayer is not an attempt to overcome God's reluctance to take action; nor can we try in prayer to make him do what we want. It is our acknowledgement that God knows best how to bring about good on earth, and when we ask for anything from God, we demonstrate that we know the true source of everything good.

As we learn to pray, we must remember that prayer is effective only if we are asking for what God wants, not expecting him to do what *we* want. **'Now this is the confidence we have in him, that if we ask anything according to his will, he hears us.'**[90] Carol J. Shewmake says, 'God has purposely limited himself in intervention in human lives in order to preserve individual freedom.' And she continues, 'When the righteous pray for family, friends, and even those they will never contact, God freely acts in the lives of those people in a way that he would not if we did not pray.'

Bringing in the Kingdom

God created human beings in the first place to have friends because he wanted fellowship, and he loved us so much that he did not want to turn us into puppets by imposing his will on us. It was, and still is, his heart-felt desire to work in partnership with human beings, to bring his Kingdom to earth, and it is this partnership which makes prayer pleasing to God and effective in the world. Everything depends on the relationship we have with him, and our understanding of his love and willingness to bring about good things in our lives when we ask.

To help us, the Father sent Jesus to be our role model.

90 1 John 5:14, NKJV

In God's time

Copying the prayers that Jesus prayed shows us what we need to know, and helps us at the same time to become like him. Some may already believe that God's Kingdom exists in heaven, but many of us struggle to believe he really wants heaven to come to earth. However, this is in fact how Jesus taught his disciples to pray: **'May your Kingdom come soon. May your will be done here on earth, just as it is in heaven.'**[91] The words from the Lord's Prayer are probably familiar, but it is worth taking time to consider deeply what they mean. It is the Father's intention to bring his will down to earth. He wants to spread his Kingdom here. So, when we do not pray according to his will, the only answer we can expect is 'No!' When we do pray for his will to be done, we know he rejoices. It is as if he is yelling, 'Well done! You understood!'

Becoming like Jesus

Of course, it is not only the world that is changed if we pray according to God's will. He also has a plan for our own lives. By praying the way Jesus prayed, we bring about positive changes in your own hearts, to become the success God has always wanted us to be. Prayer is the key to a new life and a new relationship with God. Prayer helps us to grow to the kind of spiritual maturity that Jesus had, **'attaining to the whole measure of the fulness of Christ'**[92] as the Bible puts it. It confers on us his power, and his authority to make a difference in the world, even authority over Satan. Jesus said we have been given authority **'to overcome all the power of the enemy.'**[93]

In addition, by praying faithfully, you slowly gain the stability, gentleness and peace that comes from God. The power you obtain from prayer is not a means of gaining control over other people, like the political power of those in office. God does not want you controlling people, because you cannot fix people's problems the way you fix a broken bicycle. If you try, then most

91 Matthew 6:10, NLT
92 Ephesians 4:13
93 Luke 10:19

often you end up hurting or breaking them. Jesus' teaching on prayer takes you in the opposite direction. By humbling yourself before God, by surrendering your life to him, and by asking him to take charge and fix whatever is wrong, you become less controlling, and more peaceful. Prayers help you to be calm, patient, still, and able to wait for the good things God intends for you. He exchanges all your worries and anxieties for his peace. He says, **'Come to me, all you who are weary and burdened, and I will give you rest.'**[94] The humility to recognise that God knows better than we do is a key to being effective in prayer. Indeed, God himself insists upon it, and attaches his promise to it. He says, **'If my people, who are called by my name, will humble themselves and pray and seek my face and turn from their wicked ways, then will I hear from heaven and will forgive their sin, and will heal their land.'**[95]

Prayer gives us the ability to persevere when things go wrong, or when we find ourselves in difficulties. Trials and times of testing may come, and it is then we have to choose what to believe all over again. Has God lost control? Is it all too much for him? The height of success for Jesus was not what any of us would choose for ourselves. But when Jesus wanted to accomplish his most important God-given mission he prayed, **'Father, the time has come. Glorify your Son, that your Son may glorify you. For you granted him authority over all people that he might give eternal life to all those you have given him.'**[96] If this is what Jesus did, then we should do so, too. If we want to accomplish our God-given mission, and be successful in God's time, we must pray. PUSH – **P**ray **U**ntil **S**omething **H**appens!

Being close to God

All of us hope that when we pray we will draw close to God, and that one of the benefits of prayer will be to make us holy,

94 Matthew 11:28
95 2 Chronicles 7:14
96 John 17:1-2

In God's time

as God is holy. It is reassuring to know that is exactly what God wants too, as he has shown throughout all the stories of the Bible. In the days of the Old Testament, before Jesus came to earth, God promised to be with his people as they travelled through the wilderness from Egypt. He ordered Moses to build the Ark of the Covenant, and it was there that God resided. The prayer life of the Israelites centred on this holy Ark, and the people carried it wherever they went. His presence was also seen all through the Israelites' journey in the desert as a pillar of fire at night and a cloud in daytime. This signified his role as a protector and as a light to our lives.

Later, between 982 and 962 BC, God allowed the great King Solomon to build a temple in Jerusalem. The Ark of the Covenant was placed in the 'Holy of holies', the most sacred part of the temple. Again, people would come to worship and to pray where they could be physically close to God. However, they couldn't get right up close because the 'Holy of holies' was separated from other parts of the temple by a curtain. By staying behind the curtain, God was perhaps saying to his people, 'something has come between us.' Indeed it had.

Although animal sacrifices were offered in the temple, they could never completely atone for the sins of the people. So our loving God, who wanted to be so close to his people, provided the way forward by sending his son. It was Jesus' mission on earth to die for us, so that the sins that separate us from God would be wiped away. The Bible records that at the very moment Jesus died on the cross the curtain in the temple was unaccountably torn in two from top to bottom, opening up the way into the divine presence. Indeed, Jesus is Emanuel, which means 'God with us'.

Perhaps it is hard to take this on board, because it may seem too good to be true. But because of all that Jesus has done for us, there is now absolutely nothing to separate us from God.

We can be completely intimate with him. We don't need to go to a special place to be close to him, because now we can invite him to live in our hearts. Wherever we are, God is, so close that we are one with him. He reassures us through his Word that we are **'the temple of the living God.'**[97]

By offering simple but sincere prayers in your heart in the name of Jesus, you make use of the free-phone to call the King of the Universe. There is no call barring, call waiting, or being held in a queue. Prayer can be offered without assuming a special posture or attitude, and it can be offered in any place – in the train, aeroplane, or bus, under your duvet, in the bathroom, or at the kitchen sink.

How to pray

One of the questions I encounter most of the time when I invite people to pray is: How do I pray? What shall say? How do I start? Most of us think prayer is a complex construction of sentences with big vocabularies. Prayer is speaking to God as we speak to our friends; normal conversation using simple and clear words as far as possible. I recently attended a soup kitchen run by our church community services department. After the meal, a small service is conducted and during this service I heard a prayer that really changed my perspective of prayer. One of the attendees was asked to pray and this is what he said:

Dear Jesus,

Thank you for these people attending to our needs for food. Bless us today and please give us kind enough people to give us warm duvets, shoes and warm food. You know what I mean, Jesus. Some of us have not had a cup of tea for long. You know what I mean; and, Jesus, please don't leave us in streets for long.

Amen. See you later, Jesus.

---

97 2 Corinthians 6:16

Keep it simple and from the heart

Jesus always insisted on simple models of prayer. He said, **'When you pray, do not keep on babbling like pagans, for they think they will be heard because of their many words.'**[98] Prayer should be like talking to an old friend, and no one uses long words or complicated sentences when talking to friends. God wants our prayers to be simple, but originating from our hearts. He can always tell if we are really praying to him, or whether we have secretly got our minds on impressing him, or making ourselves look good in the eyes of other people. Any attempt to show off with eloquence, loudness or length of prayer is fraudulent, and our words will never reach the heart of God that way. He does not take account of our silly attempts to make ourselves look important, holy, or humble.

Jesus told a story about a religious leader and a tax collector who went into a temple to pray. **'The Pharisee** [religious leader] **stood up and prayed about himself: "God, I thank you that I am not like other men – robbers, evildoers, adulterers – or even like this tax collector. I fast twice a week and give a tenth of all I get." But the tax collector stood at a distance. He would not even look up to heaven, but beat his breast, and said, "God, have mercy on me, a sinner." '** (Luke 18:11-13.) Jesus was quick to assure us that it was the prayer of the tax collector that was heard in heaven, and that he, not the Pharisee, left with God's blessing.

When our minds are more on ourselves than on God, we can actually forget what we were originally praying for by the time we get half way through. Or we may pray out loud for our food, and then a few minutes later ask, 'Have we prayed?' Or we may forget to pray all through the week, and then try to make up for lost time in church on Sabbath. God is never impressed. What matters to him is the sincerity in our hearts,

98 Matthew 6:7

our honesty, and our faith in him. He looks for confidence in us that he will answer according to his plan, in his time, and for his glory.

God is our Helper, so we can be absolutely certain in our minds that he is faithful and just to forgive us, and to bring us all the help we need. It is his desire to hear our prayers so we do not need to be afraid.

More prayers, more success

We have already explored how prayer can be likened to a conversation with an old friend, and we know that we do not need to use any special vocabulary, or fancy phrases. But it is also true to say that conversation with a friend would be very boring indeed if we only repeated the same few words over and over again. Talking to God can be richly varied at different times, so that the relationship stays alive and fresh, new every day. What to pray for is a question many people ask. In other words, what shall we say to God? These five different-categories of prayer can help to get us started. As time goes on we shall find more to share with God.

Prayer of gratitude

First and foremost, before we ask God for anything, we need to praise him, and to thank him for enabling us to talk to him because of all that Jesus accomplished for us on the cross. Our success in life in God's time will reach its fullness by our learning to thank him for everything. The Bible encourages Christians with these words: **'With Jesus' help, let us continually offer our sacrifice of praise to God by proclaiming the glory of his name.'**[99]

The words 'sacrifice of praise' are significant, because the act of thanking God should not depend on how you feel. God is

99 Hebrews 13:15, NLT

worthy of your praise even when you are having a bad day and everything seems to be going wrong. God's goodness, mercy, loving-kindness, grace, and long-suffering nature, have everything to do with your life. It is because of his grace that you are not consumed, and thanking him should be as natural as breathing.

When you watch television and see that millions of people suffer in different parts of the world, you get an opportunity to appreciate again the richness of your own possessions, and thank God for his abounding grace. When you see the sick, you can thank God for your own health. Thank him for listening to you, even though you go on a bit! Thank him for laughter, for classical music, for Gospel music, for ballet, for snowflakes, for whatever delights you and enriches your life and draws you closer to him. By including thanksgiving in your prayers, you add to the list of ways in which you can 'pray without ceasing', until it becomes a whole way of life. Then when the time comes for you to put away all the things of this world, you will be able not to complain, or ask why, but to offer gratitude for his presence.

It is only when you lose focus on all that God has done and continues to do for you that you fail to thank him and lack what to talk about with him. When you focus on the sacrifice he made because of his great love, you learn to look up, and be grateful.

Prayer of consecration

To consecrate something means to set it apart for sacred use, and it is a word God himself has used from earliest Old Testament times, asking his people to consecrate themselves. When you offer yourself in a prayer of consecration, you are inviting God to anoint you, and use you for a purpose of his choice, and you make yourself available to work with him by

In God's time

being ready to accept whatever he wants you to do, and to go wherever he wills. Dedicating your life and all that you are to him makes you an instrument in his hands, a tool fit for the purpose for which it was made. It allows God to use you in the best possible way.

When you truly dedicate yourself to the Lord, you simply avoid the worries and burdens of trying to run your own life. Invite him to take the lead, and just follow with the assurance of safety, of reaching your destination in his time. It is not always easy, and there may come moments of doubt. Perhaps you had a particular expectation of what you might receive from God, and it didn't happen. That is a trial that puts pressure on you to choose again. Will you still sing, ''Tis so sweet to trust in Jesus'?

Our faith may be shaken if we are not prepared to accept the strategy God uses to bring success in our lives. However, when we consecrate ourselves to God every day, we are embracing the most important ingredient of success. We are not only being true to ourselves, but also being what God wants us to be, and we will finish at the highest point destined for us in our lives.

God has a lot of work he desires to do in his people, and through them. If they set themselves apart for him, they will receive all the benefits of his blessing. He promises, **'I will make an everlasting covenant with them. I will never stop doing good to them, and I will inspire them . . . so that they will never turn away from me. I will rejoice in doing them good and will assuredly plant them in this land with all my heart and soul.'**[100]

Be ready to accept his will even when it conflicts with your desires. Hold on to your faith. As this poem says, the will of God is never unfair.

---

100 Jeremiah 32:40-41

The will of God will never take you where
The grace of God cannot keep you,
and his arms cannot support you,
the riches of God can't supply your needs,
and his power cannot endow you.

The will of God will never take you where
God's Spirit can't work through you,
or where his wisdom can't teach you,
the army of God can't protect you,
or where the hands of God cannot mould you.

The will of God will never take you where
God's love cannot enfold you;
or the mercies of God cannot sustain you,
the peace of God can't calm your fears,
or his authority cannot overrule for you.

The will of God will never take you where
the comfort of God cannot dry your tears,
or the Word of God cannot feed you,
the miracles of God can't be done for you,
or his omnipresence cannot find you.
(Author unknown)

Prayer of commitment
It is through prayers of commitment that you learn to trust the Lord, and begin to appreciate his faithfulness in love and his ability to care for all your concerns. The apostle Peter encourages you to **'Cast all your anxiety upon him because he cares for you.'**[101]

The Bible describes the relationship between God and human beings in different ways, all of which tell us something

---

101 1 Peter 5:7

about God's love and care. It is likened to a husband and his wife, to a ruler and his obedient people, to a potter and the clay, to a father and his children, and lastly to a shepherd and his sheep. The relationship is sealed in the New Testament through Jesus, who taught his disciples to address God as **'Our Father, who art in heaven',** showing how very close and intimate God desires to be with the people he created. Ellen White says that, 'Christ teaches us to address him [God] by a new name, a name entwined with the dearest associations of the human heart. He gives us the privilege of calling the infinite God our Father.'[102]

This Father-son relationship is what allows us to pray to him without fear. All our cares, burdens and worries are cast completely into his capable and caring hands. When we do this, he is faithful and intervenes in our situations, and works out solutions on our behalf. There is no limit to what we can commit to God, our personal problems, our marriage, children, parents; our church, our work and our future; we should continuously commit to him those holding us back from advancing in our spiritual well-being, and above all commit ourselves and all our cares into his hands.

A prayer of commitment can be prayed anywhere, at any time, out loud or silently in your heart. God already knows what your needs are, and he already has the answer. When you pray, you are not prompting the Almighty to create a solution to your problems, but asking that the solution he already has might be made visible to you. It is in letting go and trusting God that you learn to understand why Jesus assured his disciples, **'My yoke is easy and my burden is light.'**[103] Commit everything to him, and then look around while you wait for results. Open your eyes and ears, search for an open door, and follow the path that he directs you to.

---

102 *Christ's Object Lessons*, pages 141, 142
103 Matthew 11:30

Prayer of petition

Petition is a word that just means 'asking', but a prayer of petition is generally understood as being a prayer for yourself, asking God to fulfil your own needs. Most human beings are overly interested in themselves, but you can avoid pitfalls of selfishness in two ways. Firstly, it is not wrong to ask God to strengthen you in faith, and help you by his grace to be successful in all that you do. The focus here is your spiritual well-being, and your godly dependence on the Father's grace.

Secondly, it is important to ask the Father to help you overcome sin. The nature of sin is blind, and without the Father's help you are unlikely to see the things you do which are displeasing to him. When he sheds his light on your life in response to your request, you will be able to see more clearly the direction in which he wants you to go, and the sins he wants you to leave behind.

You can also petition the Father to shed light in the lives of people around you that you love and want to bless. At the point of his death, Jesus, our role model, prayed for the forgiveness of those who were killing him. He thought more about the benefit he could bring to others than of his own need, even in the trial of such intense pain.

Jabez was a man who led a troubled life, but his unusual, one-sentence prayer recorded in the Bible was enough to change his life completely, to enable him to move from sickness to health and, ultimately, to prosperity. **'Oh, that you [God] would bless me and enlarge my territory! Let your hand be with me, and keep me from harm.'**[104] What a perfect prayer!

Joyce Mayer says, 'It is important to petition God about our future . . . to pray and ask him for his help in allowing us to succeed.' She continues, 'Our success won't come through personal struggle or vain effort, but as a result of God's grace.'[105]

---

104 1 Chronicles 4:9, 10
105 Joyce Mayer, *How to Succeed in Being Yourself*, page 236

Prayer of intercession

According to *Chambers Dictionary*, to intercede is to act as a peacemaker between two people, or groups of people. When a human being has broken a link between himself and God, there is a breach in their relationship caused by sin, and Someone needs to place himself in the gap and pray for that person. This is the role of Jesus.

We have already seen that prayer is only effective when we are asking for things we know to be within the will of God. When we pray for others, we pray in the name of Jesus, who intercedes on our behalf with the Father, and we can be certain that he wants to restore a right relationship with every human being.

Carol J. Shewmake spells out the way in which God has made himself dependent upon the prayers of Christians to bless the world. She says that everything God gives to us has been paid for by the blood of his Son, so when we pray for others, we allow God to bless the world through us. It is fantastic! We can't all be pastors, priests, church elders, teachers or evangelists, but we can all pray and intercede for others. Just imagine for a minute what it would be like if all church members prayed constantly for those they disliked, or judged, or despised, or led into sin. How quickly the church would finish God's work, and what a tremendous blessing would result.

More than this, God wants to reach the whole world through your prayers. If you trust yourself into his hands, and reach out to the world, you will be the middleman between him and all the people in every nation. You can intercede through Jesus and talk to God about the homeless, the orphans, the widows, the poor and hungry, and the millions who have not yet heard the Good News of salvation. Every blessing going out to the world can go through you, so do not be afraid to involve yourself in the ministry of intercession. Ask, and the Holy Spirit will reveal to you whom you should pray for, and even give you the words to say.

Do not be tempted to think that your prayers will change God. But be assured that your prayers will help you to act according to his will, and will set your mind in harmony and agreement with his. Jesus prayed for others more than for himself, and he is our role model. When you pray for others, you are working in co-operation with the Great Intercessor himself, and it is the type of prayer that God delights to answer above all others. There is only one possible stumbling block to overcome, and that lies in your own heart. You cannot effectively intercede for someone you dislike, or have a grudge against, because the words you use need to be in agreement with the feelings in your heart. It is important, then, to ask God to help you forgive completely the one who has hurt you before you start praying for him or her.

Carol Shewmake says, 'Intercessory prayer turns every personal blessing received into a blessing for others.'[106] It turns you away from yourself and directs you to the needs of your fellow human beings. The more you pray for others, the more you become an unselfish person. So allow God to use you as an agent to govern the world by having a part to play in his ministry to bless the world. You will certainly be successful in his time if you help other people through prayer. Sowing seeds in the lives of others is a guaranteed way to reap a good harvest of blessing in your own.

Let me tell you a story I received via email recently. It was written by a doctor who worked in South Africa.

'One night I had worked hard to help a mother in the labour ward, but in spite of all we could do she died, leaving us with a tiny premature baby and a crying two-year-old daughter. We would have difficulty keeping the baby alive, as we had no

106 Carole J. Shewmake: *Sanctuary Secrets to Personal Prayer*, 1995 Review and Herald Publishing Association, page 21

incubator. (We had no electricity to run an incubator.) We also had no special feeding facilities. Although we live near the equator, nights were often chilly with treacherous drafts.

'One student midwife went for the box we had for such babies and the cotton wool the baby would be wrapped in. Another went to stoke up the fire and fill a hot water bottle. She came back shortly in distress, to tell me that when she was filling the bottle, it had burst. Rubber perishes easily in tropical climates. "And it is our last hot water bottle!" she exclaimed.

'As the saying from the West goes, "no good crying over spilled milk", so in Central Africa it might be considered no good crying over burst hot water bottles. They do not grow on trees and there are no drugstores down forest pathways.

' "All right", I said, "put the baby as near the fire as you safely can, and sleep between the baby and the door to keep it free from draughts. Your job is to keep the baby warm."

'The following noon, as I did most days, I went to have prayers with some of the orphanage children who chose to gather with me. I gave the youngsters various suggestions of things to pray about and told them about the tiny baby. I explained our problem about keeping the baby warm enough, mentioning the hot water bottle. The baby could so easily die if it got chills. I also told them of the two-year-old sister, crying because her mother had died.

'During the prayer time, one ten-year-old girl, Ruth, prayed with the usual blunt conciseness of our African children. "Please, God," she prayed, "Send us a water bottle. It'll be no good tomorrow, God, as the baby will be dead, so please send it this afternoon."

'While I gasped inwardly at the audacity of the prayer, she added by way of a corollary, "And while you are about it, would you please send a dolly for the little girl so she'll know you really love her?" As often with children's prayers, I was put on the spot. Could I honestly say, "Amen"? I just did not believe that God could do this. Oh, yes, I know that he can do everything. The Bible says so. But there are limits, aren't there? The only way God could answer this particular prayer would be by sending me a parcel from the homeland. I had been in Africa for almost four years, and had never, ever received a parcel from home. Anyway, if anyone did send me a parcel, who would think to put in a hot water bottle? I lived on the equator!

'Half way through the afternoon, while I was teaching in the nurses' training school, a message was sent that there was a car at my front door. By the time I reached home, the car had gone, but there on the veranda was a large twenty-two-pound parcel. I felt tears pricking my eyes. I could not open the parcel alone, so I sent for the orphanage children. Together we pulled off the string, carefully undoing each knot. We folded the paper, taking care not to tear it unduly. Excitement was mounting.

'Some thirty or forty pairs of eyes were focused on the large cardboard box. From the top, I lifted out brightly coloured, knitted jerseys. Eyes sparkled as I gave them out. Then there were the knitted bandages for the leprosy patients, and the children looked bored. Then came a box of mixed raisins and sultanas – they would make a batch of buns for the weekend. Then, as I put my hand in again, I felt a . . . could it really be? I grasped it and pulled it out – yes, a brand new, rubber hot water bottle. I cried. I had not asked God to send it. I had not believed that he could.

'Ruth was in the front row of the children. She rushed forward, crying out, "If God has sent the bottle, he must have sent the dolly, too!" Rummaging down to the bottom of the box, she pulled out the small, beautifully dressed dolly. Her eyes shone! She had never doubted. Looking up at me, she asked, "Can I go over with you, Mummy, and give this dolly to that little girl, so she'll know that Jesus really loves her?"

'That parcel had been on the way for five whole months, packed by my former Sunday school class, whose leader had heard and obeyed God's prompting to send a hot water bottle, even to the tropics. And one of the girls had put in a dolly for an African child, *five months before* – in answer to the believing prayer of a ten-year-old that afternoon.

'The Lord says, **"Before they call I will answer."** '[107]

Our God really is an awesome God!

107 Isaiah 65:24

Structuring your prayer life

Special times

Though there is no restriction in regard to praying times, it is good to set aside time for prayer. If we can manage to set aside time for our meals, surely God is pleased to hear us at special times, too, times we dedicate particularly for the purpose.

Early morning

Like many people, I don't like getting up early in the morning for anything, unless it is very important. Jesus enjoyed his sleep, too, but he also knew that the best sleep is found when you are at peace with the Father and with the world. **'The next morning Jesus woke long before daybreak and went out alone into the wilderness to pray.'**[108] What pushed Jesus out of bed? The need to set his priorities for the day! He realised how important it was to draw close to his Father before doing anything else with the day. If Jesus, the Son of the Living God, prayed in the early morning, who are we not to do the same? We cannot expect success in anything we are doing without first inviting God into our plans, and involving him all the way. This is the golden rule for structuring our prayer lives. Start with a morning prayer, and let the day flow from there.

108 Mark 1:35, NLT

In God's time

Regular intervals

Praying once a day is a starting point, but as you grow in your relationship with Jesus, you will discover that your desire to be with God grows and grows, and that prayer becomes a habit throughout the day. The prophet Daniel was in the habit of praying to God three times a day, and he didn't care who knew it. Even when a law was passed forbidding worship of anyone other than the King of Babylon, Daniel went right on worshipping God, morning, noon and night. **'He went home to his upstairs room where the windows opened toward Jerusalem. Three times a day he got down on his knees and prayed, giving thanks to his God, just as he had done before.'**[109] Daniel's habit was not an act of defiance against the king, but simply a chosen way of life, to pray three times a day.

The apostles continued as Jesus had taught them. **'They devoted themselves to . . . the breaking of bread and to prayer.'**[110] When they failed to do so, things did not go well. At times, their direction lost its focus because they found themselves 'too busy to pray', but when they realised what had happened they started delegating responsibilities to others so that they could go back to the work they were anointed to do.[111] Another example is Martin Luther, who is reported to have said, 'I have so much business I cannot get done without spending three hours a day in prayer.' This kind of attitude does not materialise overnight. It takes time and discipline to develop, and perseverance to continue when things get tough.

Pray without ceasing

Over a period of time, the more you focus on your relationship with God, talking to him becomes as natural as your heartbeat, or your breathing. It was this kind of prayer that the apostle Paul had in mind when he called on the people of Thessalonica

109 Daniel 6:10
110 Acts 2:42
111 Acts 6:1-7

to **'pray without ceasing'**.[112] It is a stage beyond allocating special times for prayer, and it is the greatest indication we have of how intimate God wants us to be with him. It is quite impossible to plead and beg with someone for a long period of time, but you can certainly chat all day. You can do it with your partner, your friends, relatives and neighbours. I talk with my wife the whole day, and we keep on talking till late at night without any effort. The same can apply with God.

Any time you remember friends, encounter a good or bad situation, or have any kind of issue during the day, talk to God about it. One of the best biblical examples of this is Enoch, who reached a stage where every heartbeat was a prayer. Because of his close relationship with God, **'Enoch was taken from this life, so that he did not experience death.'**[113] For you and me, too, prayer can become an effortless daily act.

Sabbath rest

There is another special time of prayer that must not be overlooked in structuring one's prayer life. Nothing learned from Jesus in the New Testament can contradict the Ten Commandments of the Old Testament. They will always be in harmony. By giving the Commandments, God was showing his people how to live a good life, pleasing to him. And Jesus put into practice God's commandment to 'Remember the Sabbath day by keeping keep it holy.' The Bible tells us, **'He went to Nazareth, where he had been brought up, and on the Sabbath day he went into the synagogue, as was his custom.'**[114] God makes it very clear in the Bible that he wants us to rest and take time off from our daily work. It is a command we ignore much too often, and we pay the penalty in stress-ridden lives. People either forget to take a break from work, or they take a break and then forget to pray. Neither of these failings does you any good. God set the pattern when he created the world – six days for work and one to rest. If it is good enough for God, it must be good enough for us, too.

Today, the most usual way of 'keeping the Sabbath' is to go to church to hear the Word of God and to pray in fellowship with other believers. God wants us to take time to worship him on a particular day. However, when that is not possible because of our jobs (for those in life-saving related shifts), he doesn't mind, so long as, at regular weekly intervals, we take special time away from work to be with him, to worship, to listen to him and to pray.

Special places

Ideally, the church is the right place for prayers. God said; **'My house will be called a house of prayer for all nations.'**[115] This, however, does not mean we should not pray elsewhere. Some people have places in their homes, forests, bushes or solitary areas specially reserved and dedicated for prayers. This is good, but is not necessary if we can't afford one. Following the fact that our bodies are a temple of the living God, I am confident that every prayer offered from our hearts, even without saying a word, will be heard at the throne of God. The apostle Paul tells us to pray, **'at all times in the Spirit, with all prayer and supplication. To that end keep alert with all perseverance, making supplication for all the saints.'**[116] Our personal success is built upon our sincerity and humbleness in inviting God to our activities in every place.

115 Isaiah 56:7
116 Ephesians 6:18, English Standard Version

Right plans and right direction

I don't know about you, but personally I find it very difficult to separate my ideas from God's. I suspect it is a common complaint, especially in those tricky areas of life where the Bible is silent, or does not give us any specific guidance. How do I know for sure that this is the right time to marry, or to move house, or to study in further education, or to change jobs? God says, **'I will instruct you and teach you in the way you should go.'**[117] Are you happy about this? Well, I'm not. I need a little more detail! How can I know it is God speaking, and not just my own desire, or lust, or selfishness?

To make sense of the way in which God guides you, you can begin by learning to distinguish between 'ideas' that come and go fairly quickly, and 'direction', which is a much more permanent and stable thing. Being sensitive to the difference is an important starting place in listening for the Master's voice. God is very persistent in his leading, and the direction he sets for you, and therefore you can trust him. Wait confidently for him, because he knows no delays and you can't hurry him either. His leading is consistent, and he is patient while you may have to hear what he says several times before you understand. At times your opinions may seem to clash with what God has in store for you, because like everyone else you want things your way, not according to God's will for you.

117 Psalm 32:8

In God's time

But the Lord does not give up on us. In the twenty-first century, most of our desires are gratified instantly, and we are accustomed to receiving information at the touch of a button, or more probably a mouse. But God's direction is not given in this way, and at first for most of us it may make no sense at all to a rational mind. God does not give us mere knowledge, but a revelation of himself through the Spirit, and when he leads us it is always towards himself. We cannot receive this instantaneously. One step at a time is all that God asks of us, and we need to be as gentle on ourselves as God is with us. The Psalmist says, **'If the Lord delights in a man's way, he makes his steps firm.'**[118] It is not the marathon run which is strengthened, but the single step taken in faith.

God is an escort

The second lesson in learning to discern God's leading is to remember that God does not sit on the terrace like a coach at a football match, shouting orders at you on how to play the game. You can also forget the image of a boxing trainer, who never goes into the ring but lets the boxer take all the punches. These are images of leaders who keep their distance, and make you do all the hard work yourself, but God is not like that. It becomes clear from reading the stories of Moses and the Israelites, on their journey from slavery in Egypt to freedom in the Promised Land, that our God wants to be *with* his people. **'I will be with you'**[119] was God's promise when he called Moses to the responsible and difficult work of confronting Pharaoh. As they moved through the desert **'they drank from the supernatural rock that accompanied their travels – and that rock was Christ**.'[120]

Have a look at the story in the Bible about the disciples' turbulent night at sea.[121] They were being buffeted by strong winds and waves. At about three o'clock in the morning, Jesus

118 Psalm 37:23
119 Exodus 3:12
120 1 Corinthians 10:4, Revised English Bible
121 Matthew 14:22-34

walked out to them on the water. Have you ever asked, 'What was Jesus doing in the middle of the lake at that time of night?' The only possible conclusion I can draw is that Jesus was there to be with his disciples in their hour of need. The darkest hour of the night of your problem is also your meeting point with God. He is your escort. He has created you to do something more than you are doing now, not merely to avoid failure in this life. He will escort you all the way and make sure you reach your destination.

The Spirit of God inside every human being always yearns to do the things that Jesus did, like healing the sick, feeding the hungry, or educating the ignorant. There is something that wants you to leave your comfort zone and your routine existence, and abandon yourself to the high adventure of following God. God has set today as the time for you to get out of your problem boat, and start walking on the water by reaching out to him, and being dependent on him. This book did not fall into your hands by chance. God is calling you, to awaken the giant in you.

God is in front of you

God's desire for intimacy is revealed in the way he stays alongside his people without flinching (yes, right into the boxing-ring to fight on your behalf!). But in addition to being with you, he also promises to be in front of you to light the path, to protect you, and encourage you.

You may remember the story of the three Hebrew boys who were thrown into a fiery furnace for refusing to worship King Nebuchadnezzar's golden image.[122] Before the flames could harm the boys, God was already there in the fire to take the heat himself and to protect them from death. Picture God in heaven, asking his angels which of them could make the fastest time down to earth to save the boys. 'Three seconds!' boasts

---

122 Daniel 3:13-27

In God's time

one. 'Not fast enough,' declares God. 'I can make it in one second,' calls the angel Gabriel. 'Too late! I'm already here!' sounds the voice of Jesus.

The Bible is full of stories of God going ahead of his people. Remember Daniel in the lions' den?[123] By the time the soldiers lowered Daniel down into the den, God's angel was already there to shut the mouths of the lions, and save him from certain death. God was way ahead of Moses when it came to dealing with Pharaoh, to protect him from the power wielded by the Egyptian ruler. And to bring this right up-to-date, God has shown through the cross of Jesus that he is way ahead of you, too, in dealing with all that Satan can throw at you, even death itself.

All we have to do is depend on him. He even declares, **'Apart from me you can do nothing.'**[124] And the apostle Paul had learned the same lesson when he declared, **'When I am weak, then I am strong.'**[125] I call this 'forced dependency', and it took a while for me to learn it. God deliberately leaves us in situations where we are out of your depth, precisely so that we acknowledge our own weakness, and need of his strength. Many times in our office we have seen that prayer increases our workload. When we reduce our prayer times, or the intensity of our prayers, our markets start to disappear. We know now that our employment agency runs on prayer-battery power. If it were not for God's powers, we would have been out of the market long ago.

God is behind you

I love learning about God from the lessons of nature, especially with children. Our son Neil likes to read about birds and animals, and to watch nature programmes on television. Together we discovered how eagles teach their young to fly, and were amazed to find out that God uses the image of a

123 Daniel 6:22
124 John 15:5
125 2 Corinthians 12:10

mother eagle in describing his way of encouraging us. It wasn't very comforting to begin with, but I have never yet heard of an eagle that failed to learn to fly.

Listen to this. First, the mother eagle pushes the young one out of the nest and over the cliff edge. Through fear of death, the fledgling releases its power, discovers its wings and learns to ride the currents of air. If it should falter, or fail to gain enough height, the mother eagle flies behind and below, literally carrying her young one on her own wings up to a safer height. The Bible says our Father God is **'Like an eagle that stirs up its nest and hovers over its young, that spreads its wings to catch them, and carries them on its pinions.'**[126] You may not like the discomforting thought of being pushed out of the nest, but let me tell you, God intends that you should fly, and not to be grounded by your fears. The source of your strength may stay hidden or dormant if you are afraid of flying. Will you trust him to come behind you, and lift you up if you start to fall?

Perhaps, like me, you feel uncomfortable about new beginnings. There is a tendency in human beings to feel secure in staying put with familiar surroundings (comfort zone), and the thought of a new place, new job, new church, new friends or neighbours can make them feel anxious. I remember how hard it was for me to move to a new area, for example. So many questions arose in me. But at times God may push you out of your cosy nest, in order for you to discover your hidden strengths, just like the parent eagle. It is better not to wait until God pushes, but to plan with him in readiness for the next move. You have all the resources within you, or around you, and you have God behind you to lift you up.

The race is not to the swift

Your life can be viewed as a journey, or a race set before you. I wonder if you think, as I have done in the past, that it often

126 Deuteronomy 32:11

In God's time

seems long, tiresome, serious, rough and tough, with interspersed moments of joy and excitement. It seemed to me that the laborious work tended to overshadow the good times, and the deeper I plunged into the life I had created the less excitement there was, because it had all become too predictable. I felt there was no creativity in my life, because my time off was always interrupted by unimportant, low-priority stuff. There was no time left to smell the roses. I looked around me, and sure enough in my life-management meetings I came across others who had the same problem. There were parents, for example, who had no time to enjoy the presence of their children, certainly many people who had no time to talk to God, and many men who had no time to reminisce with their wives or partners.

What had happened to us? Why were we all running a race that seemed to have no direction, no finishing line, no prize, no medal, no applause? What kind of race were we running, anyway, that had so little excitement or joy in it? I had a heap of questions I wanted to ask God, but when I did ask him, I was surprised that his response consisted of more questions, and that got me thinking!

'Who set your goals?' 'Who appointed you to do what you are doing?' 'Did you involve me in your planning?' 'Are you acting out of a need to receive approval, to please somebody else, or to keep from disappointing someone?' 'What definition of "success" are you using?'

It will come as no surprise now if I tell you the same old problems existed even for Moses. He went to God and complained he had too much to do, no time for himself, that he was always tired and exhausted, and that he felt pretty grumpy. God told him, in effect, 'Of course you're tired, but I never told you to do all that stuff!'[127] Moses needed a radical reorganisation of his priorities and God told him to shift responsibilities, share the load and start making some changes.

---

127 Numbers 11:14-17

Right plans and right direction

Like Moses, it is very easy for you to be pushed by forces outside yourself to try to do things that, in reality, you cannot do. If you are going to be successful, according to God's definition and not the world's, then you will require total commitment, and a great measure of patience. If you have ever watched athletics, you will know how often runners are caught by their excitement or impatience, and disqualified for running before the starting gun goes off. In the spiritual realm, the winners are not necessarily the fastest runners, but those who run with patience, first getting used to the track, then planning the route and understanding where to increase speed and where to relax. On the road to life, you can choose to follow the One who has passed along the route before you. Jesus went all the way to the grave and came back. He not only knows the way; he *is* the Way.

If you are going to be productive, your energy needs to be harnessed. Draw your plans well, understand your vision, be focused on God, and take steady steps, one at a time. Steady motion means you are patient, but relentless in your progress towards your God-given goals. Watch the drivers on the road who hoot and overtake at high speed, despite all risks to other people's lives. Have you ever caught up with them two minutes later at the next red light?

'I have seen something else under the sun: The race is not to the swift or the battle to the strong, nor does food come to the wise or wealth to the brilliant or favour to the learned; but time and chance happen to them all.'[128] This wisdom from the Bible is thought to come from King Solomon, but, whoever the author was, it is certainly true, and reminds us to trust God for the direction of our lives. Failure to do so means we are easily distracted by the worries and demands of this world, or unbalanced by the trials that inevitably come.

With God in control, you can trust that everything that

128 Ecclesiastes 9:11

comes to you can be treated as a training exercise in the race. He tests your ability to stay on course, and provides you with the necessary training for your highest calling. The schedules you keep will improve you physically, mentally, spiritually and emotionally. After a while you will be able to look back and smile at some of the life obstacles you have overcome. At the time, they may have seemed insurmountable, but with hindsight you will be able to laugh at them. God allows you to be stretched in your thinking, tested in your faith, and proven in your ability to love, so that you are fit to live with him and work for him. He will plan your exercise programme for you if you invite him to, and in his time you will receive all that you need, so be patient. Learn to concentrate on the lessons God is teaching you today, and let go of worrying about everything else.

A sixteenth-century Anglican bishop said, 'In my youth, my imagination had no limits. I dreamed of changing the world. But when I grew older and wiser, I found that the world would not change, so I decided to change my country. But it, too, seemed immovable. So as I grew into my twilight years, in one last attempt, I settled for changing my family, but alas, they would have none of it. Now on my death bed I realise that if I had only first changed myself, then by example I might have changed my family, and *through* my family changed my country, and through my country changed the world.'

It is sometimes hard to believe that God intends to bring good out of the trials you are going through. This means you may have times of doubting his goodness when bad things happen. But however hard it may seem, God has promised it will work out if you trust him. **'And we know that in all things God works for the good of those who love him.'**[129] So be patient. The hard times will result in blessings in his time, and there are promises to hold on to in the meantime. The apostle Paul reminds us that our trials equip us for the future, **'so that**

129 Romans 8:28

we may be able to comfort those who are in any trouble.'[130] They increase our need of God, and can be used to develop trust in him. Anything that helps us to turn to God and lean harder on him is a blessing. We must keep moving in faith and in his grace because he alone knows his purpose for us, a purpose of well-being and not misfortune. If we invoke him and pray, he will listen to us, and if we seek him we shall find him. (See Jeremiah 29:11, 12.)

When a marriage fails, when we lose a loved one, when we find ourselves without work, or our health lets us down, we must stick with God. He knows well enough that we tend to look for him more when we are down than in the times when everything is going well and we feel fine. He is patient with our human nature and gives us his Word as a promise. **'Do not throw away your confidence [in the Lord]; it will be richly rewarded.'** (Hebrews 10:35.) What we are going through today is part of his plan to shape us and to strengthen our faith in him. We are not the first in that kind of situation.

Take Sarah for example. It is hard to know the feelings of a woman who struggles to get a child when her age seems to be against her. It is hard to understand her feelings when she goes past other women and they burst into laughter. You cannot imagine her feelings when a little girl goes to her and asks, 'Where are your children so that I can play with them?' I can guess that Sarah had a terrible time, thinking, 'O God, why can't you let me hold a little baby of mine just for one time?' I can hear her adding, 'God, don't let me miss my destiny.'

This is what I would like to pray daily: 'God, don't let me hope for things that are not part of your plan for my life. Let me hear your voice guiding me, reassuring me and telling me you love me. Give a fresh glimpse of your promise to me so that I can light with faith and take hold of it. Help me to understand the difference between what I must go after and what I must

130 2 Cor. 1:4, NKJV

wait on you for. When it is up to me, give me the strength to demolish doubt and march fearlessly into the new day you have prepared for me. When it is up to *you*, give grace and patience to wait; fill me with the joyful anticipation that accompanies a perfectly timed present.

'Lord, remind me not to "*throw away my confidence, for it will be richly rewarded.*" '

Trusting his leadership

God's leadership for your destination

With all that happens to us in life, and with all the distractions that this world offers us, it is so easy to miss our true destination. Fortunately for us, Jesus keeps calling, to remind us where we should be going. He makes us check our destination against the one he has planned for us, and he tells us whether we are on the right track for his highest calling.

I remember an incident one day when a member of our staff was sent to work in Henley-on-Thames. She took the right bus, and even got to Henley. But the route the bus took was unfamiliar to her, and she didn't see any landmarks that she recognised along the way. This poor lady continued sitting on the bus as it drove straight through Henley, right out the other side of it, and on to the next town, called Marlow. Man, was she ever late for work! Life can be like that sometimes. Just when you think you know what you're doing, you find yourself off-track, in a place you never intended to visit. Sometimes it is your own fault, and sometimes it is just a mistake. When you have no leader in your life you will often face such situations.

Have you recognised your life's final destination yet? Perhaps like the lady on the bus you feel sure you are somewhere on the way to the right destination, but for the moment you are lost. Maybe you started well, but at some point you lost track of where you were going, and why.

When Moses brought the whole nation of Israel out from Egypt, the people marvelled at God's awesome power. They were so excited because they had been freed from slavery, and they knew for sure that their destination was the Promised Land. However, as time passed, they lost their sense of direction, and fell into grumbling about the journey and how long it was taking. Maybe they started to believe they would never get there. They turned away from God, worshipped idols, and became more concerned about their day-to-day comfort than in reaching their final destination. Did God really know what he was doing after all? Could his leadership be trusted? They began to doubt it. Out of the original multitude of 600,000 that left Egypt, only two men ever reached their destination, and Moses was not one of them. The approximately two-week journey had taken forty years, and all but two had died. These two, Caleb and Joshua, were the only ones who had consistently trusted God's leadership in getting them to their proper destination.

Stephen Covey, in his book *Seven Habits of Highly Effective People,* says, 'It is incredibly easy to work hard at climbing the ladder of success, only to find out that it is leaning against the wrong wall.' If the ladder is not leaning against the right wall, then every step we take only helps us to get to the wrong top faster. But if we trust God for setting the destination, and we persist in trusting his leadership, then we get there. **'Some lost their way in desert waste lands; they found no path to a city to live in. . . . They cried to the Lord . . . He led them by a straight and easy path until they came to a city where they might live'** (Psalm 107:4-7, REB).

It doesn't depend on our knowledge of the route, but on our trust in God's leading. Bob Gass tells a story of a missionary who got lost in a jungle. He decided the best course of action would be to walk in a straight line, and finally after many hours he came to a village, and asked one of the village men to lead him to the mission station. The man started walking, and the missionary asked, 'Which way do we go?"' The man replied, 'Just follow me.' After several more hours of hacking through the jungle, the missionary still had that same sense of being lost, and let his anxiety and impatience take over. 'Are you sure this is the way?' he asked. 'How do you know?' The guide, who was used to the jungle and had made his way through it many times, gave this reassurance, 'In the jungle there is no path. I am the path. Just follow me!'

Sometimes we feel lost, and we forget where we are heading. If you feel that way too, then remember what Jesus said about trusting him for your destination. **'I am the way and the truth and the life.'**[131] His work is to keep you from making the wrong move or heading in the wrong direction. He promised that along unfamiliar paths, he would guide you. Everyone who seeks him can be sure he will point them in the right direction.

God's leadership in the details

I was asked recently to go to the Crown Court in Reading, for the trial of a man I knew. I did so because the man had attended quite a large number of our church meetings, during which he had made up his mind to follow Jesus. He had chosen the right destination, and we all thought he was ready to trust God for his leadership. However, what the man had not fully understood was that God not only leads by setting the final destination; he also wants to lead in every detail of our everyday lives.

The man had become a Christian, but he was still trying to manipulate people for his own short-term goals. Although he was already married, he had become involved in an illicit rela-

---

131 John 14:6

tionship with a woman for their mutual advantage — there was to be financial gain on one side, and a promise of immigrant status on the other. The relationship had inevitably turned sour, and the woman decided to take revenge by coaching her eleven-year-old daughter to make accusations of indecent assault against him. He was innocent of the charge, and was acquitted for lack of evidence, but it is worth remembering that he would not have ended up in court at all if he had followed God's leadership in every detail of his life.

The Bible is full of wisdom concerning the way God wants people to live, and his advice on how to make relationships that are loving, supportive, and long term. He gives us guidelines at every stage of our lives, and in many different circumstances that we may encounter along our journey. If I were to list them here, the examples would fill another book, but there is no need. Let us equip ourselves instead with the Word of God, and follow his leadership in the small details of our lives, because they are not unimportant. Moses told Joshua, **'Be strong and very courageous. . . . Obey all the law. . . . Do not turn from it . . . that you may be successful wherever you go.'**[132] There is no substitute for obedience, consistency, discipline and perseverance.

His leadership in tough times

Following Jesus gives us no assurance that the way forward will be plain sailing. If we have hope of an easy ride in our journey, then we shall surely be disappointed, because the Word of God promises that trials will come, and that we can expect them with certainty. God's love will always be with us, and surviving the hard times successfully means not doubting that fact.

If you are anything like me, though, fear may still be present, even if you do not doubt God's love. I remember a time when our family had only thirteen days to go before the lease on our

132 Joshua 1:7

house expired and we had to get out. My eldest daughter Cheryl was preparing for her exams at the same time, and back home everyone was expecting me to help by sending money. My sister wanted a good suit for her graduation, and others blamed me for not sending them tickets to come over to England for a visit. Just two months earlier I had been assisting the homeless to find places to sleep, but the project did not go well and, to finish me off, I had to face the possibility of home-lessness myself. I felt I would have been all right on my own, or just with my wife, but I ached at the thought of disrupting the children's lives.

'O God, where are you? Have you forsaken us? Am I standing in the wrong place, where your blessings are not available? Have I put my ladder against the wrong wall?' These were the kinds of prayers I was praying at the time. But the Bible is not misleading, and despite my feelings I kept assuring myself of the promises. **'At the proper time we will reap a harvest if we do not give up.'**[133]

'It never rains, but it pours', as the saying goes. To add to my troubles I received two parking tickets, and a speeding fine, which took a further £80 out of my pocket. Of course, it was nothing to do with God. It was my own fault, but it added to all my frustrations and fears. It is at times like these that you cannot afford to follow your feelings, because they only lead you deeper and deeper into depression. Instead, I chose to go out and participate in a church project to collect money in the streets for the needy, trusting God's leading for my own needs, and working to help the needs of others. God always gives us the choice whether to quit or to persevere, and he is faithful to help us if we choose the latter.

I once watched a television documentary showing the route that Dr David Livingstone took in his endeavour to spread the Gospel to remote parts of Africa. He had to endure severe

---

133 Galatians 6:9, NLT

trials, hunger and thirst and many hardships, in order to accomplish his goal. He could easily have quit in the toughest places where the bush was so thick it was nearly impossible to break through, but quitting was not in his nature. He pressed on until he reached Lake Tanganyika, trusting God to lead him through all the discomfort. When other missionaries asked him if there was a road so that they could follow in his footsteps, he replied, 'Those wanting to come can come even if there is no way.'

Whatever your personal trials may be, you can be sure that God is in them with you. Praying about them, and asking for God's leadership in your discomfort, will give you guidance on what to do. Sometimes, as with my parking and speeding fines, you have to admit that discomfort is the result of your own mistakes, and the only thing to do is own up. Occasionally hard times are allowed by God to test your faith. This, however, does not allow you to put yourself in trouble by breaking government rules, society regulations, or violating health principles.

His leadership is available in all areas of life, including times when we are waiting for something. We live in times of instant everything. Patience seems to be a vocabulary of the past. Remember, when talking about patience, Moses told Joshua, **'Be strong and very courageous. Obey all the law. . . . Do not turn from it . . . that you may be successful wherever you go.'** (1:7.) There is no substitute for obedience, consistency, discipline, and perseverance. God's time to fill us may be affected by one of these ingredients. **'Don't get tired of doing what is good. Don't get discouraged and give up, for we will reap a harvest of blessing at the appropriate time.'**[134] Waiting is hard, but when led by God we learn to wait, as we trust that he will do or give what we are waiting for.

His leadership is very important when you are in search of

---

134 Galatians 6:9, NLT

resources required for whatever you are doing. God can send you to particular people or places of help to you. Remember what Jesus told the disciples, as they required a place for the Passover supper? **'As soon as you set foot in the city a man will meet you carrying a jar of water. Follow him. . . . He will show you a large room upstairs all set out.'** (Luke 22:10, 11, REB.)

'The Lord is my shepherd. . . . He leads me . . . . Goodness and love unfailing will follow me all the days of my life.' (Psalm 23, REB.)

Enemies of God's timing

Impatience

Following the path of life God's way does not necessarily come easily or naturally to most people, because the human cultures we have developed are so often in conflict with the way God leads. This world does not teach us to be patient. We feel comfortable in a 'Now!' culture, microwaving food to eat instantly, tumble-drying our clothes, DHL-ing our parcels and emailing our correspondence. We like our shopping and banking to be drive-thru, and even our marriages are quickly made and almost as quickly disposed of when they don't turn out as we would wish.

How many of you go as far as honking your horn when the traffic lights change and the guy in front doesn't move quite fast enough? Robert Levine, in his book *The Geography of Time*, has a way of allocating units of time. He suggests that the time between the traffic light turning amber and the movement of your car before being horn-honked is the smallest unit of time, and should be called one honko-second! Jesus understands our inability to wait, and in most of the miracles described in the Bible you will find the word 'immediately' describing what happened. Jesus never goes beyond one honko-second to come to your rescue. His actions are discerning, swift and decisive. So it is not his slowness that creates a need for us to develop patience.

However, an ability to wait is a necessary virtue in becoming successful. If you want to follow God's way it is important to know that, at some juncture in life, you will be called upon to learn patience. The process helps you develop an understanding of yourself as a creature, unable alone to bring about quickly what you hope for. I am not talking about a few seconds or minutes of waiting at a bus stop, in a doctor's surgery or at the bank counter. I am talking about the kind of waiting that is more serious and perhaps painful. Sometimes waiting can bring stresses and strains to the point of mental breakdown. It is the kind of waiting the apostle Paul wrote about, saying, **'We ourselves, who have the firstfruits of the Spirit, groan inwardly as we wait eagerly for our adoption as sons, the redemption of our bodies. For in this hope we were saved. But hope that is seen is no hope at all. Who hopes for what he already has? But if we hope for what we do not yet have, we wait for it patiently.'**[135]

I am talking about the waiting of a single woman aged say thirty-five, who hopes God might give her a husband but who is beginning to despair; or the waiting of a childless couple who have been trying to start a family for more than ten years but without success, despite medical advice, IVF treatment and prayers. Think of the waiting experienced by an elderly and lonely man in a nursing home, seriously ill and longing to die, or the innocent inmate in a Texan jail awaiting appeal against a sentence of death, with clemency hanging in the hands of George Bush. These are examples of serious waiting.

Forty-three times in the Old Testament people were commanded to wait on the Lord, but why? With all his power, and the ability to do things immediately, why doesn't God give us the answers we long for, relief from our pain, and change in our

135 Romans 8:23-25

In God's time

distressing circumstances? Why do we have to wait for Jesus to come again? He said, 'I am coming soon,' and we say, 'Amen! Come, Lord Jesus.' The answer, as Ben Patterson has explained, is that what God does while you are waiting is just as important as the thing you are waiting for. So wait!

Joseph had a dream that his older brothers would bow down to him and serve him, and he was impatient for that to happen. With a total absence of tact, he told his brothers and parents about the dream. His tactlessness caused him severe suffering and separation from his family for more than twenty years. He might not have had to endure such pain if he had just decided to wait patiently, because the vision the Lord gave him came to fruition at the time that God appointed, and not a moment sooner for all his striving.

'When your endurance is fully developed, you will be strong in character and ready for anything.'[136] It is worth a glance at what the Lord did for *Jacob* while he, too, was waiting. Follow the story through in the Bible, and you will find Jacob's character altered, and the reflections in his mind taking on a more mature and measured tone. As Jacob journeyed home from his years of refuge at Laban's house, the road was surely hot and rough. The man, once headstrong and impatient, was by then considerate and thoughtful. **'I will lead on slowly, at the pace of the livestock . . . and . . . of the children.'**[137]

These stories are not just isolated biblical cases. You will find that God works exactly the same way today, and we have modern examples of businessmen and political heroes who have cherished hope of success through years of patient waiting. George Eastman made 471 experiments before he made a photographic film and found success only at the 472nd attempt, finally giving birth to the Eastman-Kodak Company. Nelson Mandela never lost his vision for justice, and his endurance

136 James 1:4, NLT
137 Genesis 33:14, 15

through years of waiting produced a strength and greatness of character that earned him deep respect across the globe.

The past

In the film, *The Lion King*, Simba the lion cub is heard to complain, 'The past hurts.' He was remembering the betrayal by his jealous uncle, and the sad death of his loving father. No one who has come through bad experiences will tell you otherwise – the past can indeed hurt very badly. But dwelling on the pain of past hurts can bind you into negative thinking, which is highly destructive. If you give it space, it will quickly distract you from your vision or dream of success.

In the Bible story of Joseph, we find that he, too, suffered from such a hurtful past. But note carefully the way he managed to hold fast to his vision, and refused to allow his mind to dwell on the way his brothers betrayed him into slavery, the false accusations of illicit sex by Potiphar's wife, and his subsequent wrongful imprisonment. Joseph had many reasons to feel resentment and bitterness because of his past, but instead he worked on his dream. In God's time, he reached his destiny by becoming one of the most powerful men in Egypt.

It is not just the pain of the past that can hold you back, but also the desire to stay in, or go back to, some happier past times. A moment of exhilaration, joy, or personal success cannot last forever, and it is wrong to try to relive it again and again in your mind's eye. All the positive experiences of the past must be treated as stepping-stones towards your ultimate goal, as fuel to light your path to the future. Jesus' disciple, Peter, would have loved to stay for ever on the mountainside where he watched in wonder as the Lord was transfigured in glory, revealing all the majesty and power of his divine nature. But Peter, like the rest of us, had to let go the passing revelation, come down from the mountain top, and soldier on through more mundane times, on the way to becoming the person God was making him into.

There is a right way to deal with the past that will neither hold you back in negative thinking, nor delude you by tempting you to cling to the good times. You can find it in the Bible, and adopt it as a guiding principle for your life, so that you move forward consistently towards your goal in God's time. When you look back and remember good times, give thanks to God for all that he has done for you. When you look back and remember hurts, remember that Jesus died so that you could be forgiven. Then forgive others as you have been forgiven, and trust Jesus for the future.

I read a verse that shook me. It says, **'Long before we first heard of Christ . . . he had his eye on us, had designs on us for glorious living.'**[138] This means that God has an assignment for each one of us to fulfil, and if we ask him, he will reveal it to us. **'If it seems slow, wait patiently, for it will surely take place.'**[139] God will not give your dream to somebody else.

It is possible that your dream will seem bizarre, impossible or irrational to others because they, not you, are caught in the past. Perhaps they have known you the way you used to be, and cannot imagine the future that God has in store for you. But do not let their lack of vision impede your progress. Those who knew Jesus as a child could only view him as the son of the local carpenter. They failed to appreciate his calling from God, and were unable to witness the miracles he was able to perform elsewhere. So beware! Discouragement may come if you share your dream with the wrong people, but success is for you if you do not let your past, or theirs, get in your way.

Quitting

We have already said much in earlier chapters about the temp-

138 Ephesians 1:11, *The Message*
139 Habakkuk 2:3

tation to quit in moments of discouragement, and the Golden Rule is quite simply, 'Don't!' Don't give up until you are absolutely convinced that God himself wants to give you a different mission and direction. As James says, **'Perseverance must finish its work so that you may be mature and complete, not lacking anything.'**[140]

When the appointed time came for God to deliver the children of Israel from the bondage of slavery in Egypt, God called Moses as their leader. You must remember that it took no fewer than eighty years to prepare Moses for this task, and even then he was not ready, wanting instead to quit before he had even begun his assignment. Listen to what Moses said to God, **'Who am I, that I should go to Pharaoh?'** and **'Lord, I have never been eloquent . . . I am slow of speech.'**[141]. Do not underestimate yourself when God has told you to do something, because the God who gives you the mission is the same God who enables you to carry it through to completion. So address the enemy inside yourself who quits at the starting line. Remember the promise set for you, **'The Lord your God goes with you; he will never leave you nor forsake you.'**[142]

At times, you may be tested to the limit. But whatever your problem, God has already gone ahead of you, and the solution is waiting in his time. You will require hope and courage, which are elements of faith, if you are going to survive days of dark despair that could tempt you to quit. But don't give up! It is darkest before the morning light breaks in, and if you are disheartened then the sure remedy is, 'Wait upon the Lord.'

Fear

The number of times the Bible says, 'Fear not', in one form of words or another, is 365. It is as if God recognises that we face fear every day of the year. People who are unaware of God's love for us, and who do not know the scriptures, tend to labour

---

140 James 1:4
141 Exodus 3:11; 4:10
142 Deuteronomy 31:6

under the misapprehension that the Bible is full of instructions like 'Don't tell lies', or 'don't commit adultery', and so on. But God knows us and loves us so deeply that the words he repeats to us most often are, 'Do not be afraid.'

Why is fear such a big issue that our heavenly Father needs to repeat his encouragement to us again and again? People in church don't seem to regard being afraid as a very serious offence, and fear has never made it to the list of the seven deadly sins. I have never heard of anyone being thrown out of his community or church fellowship for having been afraid. So what is God on about?

God wants us not to be afraid because he knows our abilities far better than we do. He created us in the first place, and he put our potential into us. That potential on its own may seem very small in our eyes, and we are always tempted to play it down. We lack courage, and refuse to step forward and take risks. But when we align ourselves with God's will, and ask in faith for his potential to work through us for his glory, then we become unstoppable in whatever we are engaged.

Jesus' disciples had all the same problems of fear that we experience today. Like Gulliver tied down by gossamer-thin threads, they were giants unable to move for fear. As the soldiers advanced to arrest Jesus in the Garden of Gethsemane, the disciples quickly forgot their leader's divine nature, and instead relied on their own strength with swords to protect themselves. After the arrest, they fled like cowards into the darkness, denying they ever knew the man who was God. Yes, Jesus' disciples were just ordinary men, scared out of their wits because they did not see themselves the way God saw them. So what happened?

It was not a sudden burst of adrenalin that enabled them to overcome their fears. Rather, it was submission to the power of the Holy Spirit of God. Instead of trusting in their own abilities, they made themselves available to God for his potential to work through them. Then, devoted to the truth, and committed to becoming what God had originally created them to be, they were able to overcome their fears and do extraordinary and supernatural things.

Your becoming a Christian does not mean your fears will all disappear overnight. But as you acknowledge your fears and place them in God's hands, he is able to transform your life, so that you dare to take risks and launch out in new adventures. It is the opposite of the kind of modern insanity that most people live with, in which they do the same things over and over again, hoping always for different results. When God commands us to be unafraid, he is not addressing our instinctive fear of danger. The fear that stops us from putting our hands in fire or from making pets out of lions and poisonous snakes is entirely healthy. But the kind of worry about life that belittles us – and paralyses us out of all motivation to move – is a parasitic tenant in the heart that has to be evicted before it eats its host!

What do you want for your life? Is it a good wife? A better job? Are you hoping to quit drugs or alcohol? If you want to progress, then face your fears, move out of your comfort zone and step into the deep with Jesus. Stop wasting your time by going round and round in circles, but seek God and let him change you. The fastest way to evict the worry parasite is to face your fears head on, with God to help you. In the quiet of your heart, tell God exactly how you feel and what you want to achieve. Acknowledge all your weakness, and tell him you know you always fail on your own. Then invite him in to give you his own courage and strength. When you do this repeatedly to overcome little fears, you will get stronger and stronger, eventually being able to conquer greater fears.

With God, you can stand up to any person, task or situation

that intimidates you, and you will be surprised how good it feels. Make the phone call you have avoided making, and take responsibility for yourself, expressing your opinion to those with whom you have previously felt shy. Do not try to placate or impress people, but instead be frank and open to the truth within you. Your 'what if?' questions will soon disappear.

Fear is a monster, capable of coming between us and our destiny in God. Ever since Adam first hid from God, stopping the flow of authentic love and intimacy, countless generations of people have hidden in fear, losing out on their true identity causing relationships to be shallow and meaningless. We hide our pain, anger, envy and hatred behind superficial smiles, all because we fear either rejection from others or the deep embarrassment of admitting the truth about our real feelings. When we hide in fear, God continues to call to us, just as he did to Adam, 'Where are you?' Unless we risk letting go, and allowing the love of God to flood into our darkness, we shall never know the power God has to set us free. Today's fearful 'What if?' questions eventually turn into the unbearable 'What might have been?' My advice is not to wait for that day, but to find out now what we can become by trusting God.

Temptation

Jesus says, **'Watch and pray so that you will not fall into temptation. The spirit is willing, but the body is weak.'** (Matthew 26:41.) But what exactly is the temptation that Jesus was so keen for us to avoid? At the centre of all that Jesus did and said on earth was his love of the Father, and his desire for people to know God. Anything that takes us away from this can be regarded as a temptation. It might be troubles, hurts, or disappointments that stop us from believing that God has good plans for us. But it could equally well be a run of good luck that causes us to believe we have no need of God, but can do just as well in our own strength. The trick is to recognise temptation, and patiently and prayerfully come back to the Father, giving thanks that our lives are in his hands.

Temptation is inevitable, but how you deal with it is what really counts. You cannot run away from the challenges, nor can you stop the devil from approaching you to upset your relationship with God. However, you can protect yourself by learning the principles God has given you for dealing with the situation, and remember, 'In each temptation there is a way out.'[143]

The first principle is to read your Bible. It gives you perspective and keeps you clear-headed. When you claim God's promises for your own, problems reduce to a manageable size, and you prevent slight irritations from becoming high dramas. The unfailing love of God never ends, and never wears out. 'Great is his faithfulness; his mercies begin afresh each day.'[144] Just when you think it is all over, or fear you won't make it, you need to let the light of his promise come like a strong beam through the fog, dispelling the darkness and letting you know that all is well because God is in ultimate control. The Word of God gives you a hope transplant, and it is wise to take it in daily.

Next, to steer through the sea of temptation, you need to focus your mind consistently on the best and not the worst. When the road is rocky and rough, learn to look up, because your heavenly Father is watching over you. Look up at the solutions, not down at the problems, because God has his own purposes behind every trouble you face in life, which will develop your character and bring out the best in you. 'For our light and momentary troubles are achieving for us an eternal glory that far outweighs them all.'[145] You do not need to resign passively in the face of severe trials or suffering. Rather, exercise control of your attitude so that your behaviour does not cause

143 See 1 Corinthians 10:13
144 Lamentations 3:23, NLT
145 2 Corinthians 4:17

offence to God or to other people. As the apostle Paul counsels us, **'Suffering produces perseverance; perseverance, character; and character, hope.'**[146] From God's perspective, what happens outwardly in the circumstances of your life is not nearly as important as what happens inside your heart. He knows that circumstances change, but your character is something that will last forever.

Get into the habit of giving thanks to God for every little detail of goodness in your life, even when things look bad. This way, when the trials are over and things start to go well again, it will feel natural to see them as blessings from the Lord. You will not be in danger of forgetting him in the good times.

Jesus is your role model in dealing with all temptations. In the good times, he soared high in the Spirit, and no one could match him. He turned water into wine; he calmed the storm at sea; he healed leprosy and straightened bent backs. But the trials were many – he cried over the defiance of Jerusalem, was frustrated with the slow quarrelsome disciples, and endured opposition from religious leaders. Things seemed tougher than life had promised, but he never stopped running his set course and he gave thanks continually to his Father. Then came a time when, at only thirty-three years of age, he could soar no more, run no more; indeed, he could barely walk. Though innocent he was flogged as a criminal and forced to carry his own cross to the place of execution. With a crown of thorns on his brow, and falling under the weight of the cross, he still continued to put one foot in front of the other, trusting the Father's will for his life and giving thanks for his love. In ways no human can fully understand, Jesus took to himself the brokenness of the human race, and bore the pain of it all in his death on the cross. Jesus paid the price for it, and all he asks of you is that you keep walking and don't give up.

---

146 Romans 5:3, 4

Believing and receiving

I have called this chapter 'Believing and receiving' to emphasise the two distinct and separate elements to be understood and grasped if you are truly to follow your highest destiny in God. The words have often been misunderstood, or used interchangeably, so it is worth unpacking them to avoid any muddled thinking.

The first is believing. **'Like clay in the hands of the potter, so are you in my hand.'**[147] God's reassurance to you is that he can make your life into something beautiful, no matter how you see yourself. Do you really believe this?

What *is* believing? Michael Losier, an American Law of Attraction Coach and Practitioner, defines it as 'the absence of doubt'. God searches the planet for anyone who is prepared to accept, with childlike simplicity, that his Word is absolutely true. Jesus said, **'I praise you, Father, Lord of heaven and earth, because you have hidden these things from the wise and learned, and revealed them to little children.'**[148] On another occasion, surrounded by children, he spoke to the adults, saying, **'I tell you the truth, unless you change and become like little children, you will never enter the kingdom of heaven.'**[149]

So ask yourself again, are you willing to accept simply, like a child, that God loves you, and is able to make something

147 Jeremiah 18:6
148 Matthew 11:25
149 Matthew 18:3

In God's time

amazing and beautiful out of your life – not in *your* idea of time, but in *his*? If you have learned from your parents and through your schooling to believe only what can be scientifically tested, it will not be easy to let go of your ideas. But remember, God is not only bigger than science – he invented it. If you admire the machinery, then you have to give credit to the engineer. Perhaps you have got as far as thinking you would very much like God to love you and transform your life, or even that you hope he can. Keep going. The next step has to be a decision to believe.

Believing means letting go of our own idea of time. God exists outside human concepts of time, and belief in him consists of trusting him like little children. Failure to believe in God's Word lengthens the journey time to our God-given destination.

God tells us he is like a potter, who is moulding us, the clay, until we become what he wants us to be. Let go of what you feel you can become, and trust the One who is outside time and who has heavenly purposes for your life. ' **"For I know the plans I have for you," says the Lord, "plans to prosper you and not to harm you, plans to give you hope and a future."** '[150] Your only responsibility is to believe it.

But it may surprise you to know that, although believing God's plan is vital to you, by itself it is not enough. **'Even the demons believe . . . , and shudder.'**[151] So believing God exists and has love at the centre of all he does is clearly not what makes you a Christian. What is lacking is the second of our two conditions for success, receiving. **'Yet to all who received him, to those who believed in his name, he gave the right to become children of God.'**[152]

Receiving the truth is an activity, separate and distinct from believing, and it involves a decision made by your will. The apostle Paul makes this clear in his letter to the Thessalonians, when he talks about **'those who perish, because they did**

150 Jeremiah 29:11
151 James 2:19
152 John 1:12

not receive the love of the truth, that they might be saved.'[153] But, when addressing the Colossian Christians, he says, 'You received Christ Jesus as Lord.'[154]

This distinction between believing and receiving is not as complicated or difficult as it may seem at first. Imagine, for instance, believing that the medicine the doctor prescribes will make you better, but then failing to swallow the tablets.

Belief has to be confirmed by action, and the success of your life is dependent upon your taking action to receive Christ into your heart. This takes the form of a prayer, in which you thank Jesus for his saving work on the cross, ask him to wash you clean from all your sin by his blood, and invite him to come and live inside your heart. This act of receiving Christ, following your confession of belief in him, is all it takes to start you down the road of Christianity on your way to success in God's time.

Believe, receive and then trust God to follow through on his promise to make something beautiful out of your life. The moment you become a Christian, God invites you to step into his peace. He offers you rest, and promises that he will work for you. Whatever hardships you face, however boxed in you feel, no task is too big for your God.

There are two stories to encourage you from God's Word. The first is the story of the Hebrews' flight from slavery in Egypt in the book of Exodus. With the Egyptian army in pursuit behind them, and the way ahead blocked by the Red Sea, they thought all was lost and death seemed certain. Then God spoke through their leader Moses. ' "Do not be afraid. Stand still, and see the salvation of the Lord, which he will accomplish for you today." '[155] God will part the waves of your Red Sea, if you are willing to step back in trust and give him control of the situation.

The second is found in the Second Book of Chronicles, which details the history of the Israelites as they learned to rely on

153 2 Thessalonians 2:10, NKJV
154 Colossians 2:6
155 Exodus 14:13, NKJV

In God's time

God. Under their leader, Jehoshaphat, the Israelites were facing the combined military forces of the Ammonites and Moabites. **'You will not need to fight in this battle?** the Lord promised. **'Position yourselves, stand still and see the salvation of the Lord'**[156] God, who loves his children, delivered them yet again. He worked while they stood still.

It is not easy in a restless world to be still and rely on God. It requires great personal discipline, especially in a crisis, but it is a discipline worth cultivating because from time to time our lives may depend upon it. God doesn't ask us to do nothing, or to give up work and family responsibilities, but he calls us to be still and quiet in our hearts and put our trust in him, whatever is happening. If we crave balance and an inner sense of peace amid a world of decadence and disorder, we would do well to heed God's commands. **'Meditate within your heart on your bed, and be still. . . . put your trust in the Lord.'**[157] You will be surprised the extent to which others will look to you for encouragement and leadership if you exude the inner peace that comes from being still before God in prayer.

It is simply a better way of living. If politicians and the leaders of nations would seek God and follow his commandments, the results would be amazing. Everywhere in the world people are in need of peace and a better life, rather than living in fear of law-breakers. It is the responsibility of every individual to adopt God's ways for himself, but we also have a collective responsibility for all our neighbours and friends, for our communities and our nations. We can help them receive Christ as we have received him. Of course, in an ideal world, the example would come from the top, from the heads of state, kings, elected leaders, councillors and governors – like King Jehoshaphat in Biblical times, who enabled his princes to help with the instruction in the law of God. It is said that, **'they went**

156 2 Chronicles 20:17, NKJV
157 Psalm 4:4, 5, NKJV

throughout all the cities of Judah and taught the people.' Jehoshaphat reigned for twenty-five years in peace, because *'the fear of the Lord fell on all the kingdoms of the lands that were around Judah.'*[158] He stood the test because he prayed and exercised his faith diligently. Don't you wish there were more leaders today calling for a return to godly ways among the people?

If the transforming power of God can evict fear, worry and bad habits from the life of an individual, then in community the same power can push away the evils that currently inhabit our public and social life.

Believe, receive, and trust God for the success of your life. Your own change of heart, the peace you find within, and the joy you experience from being loved – these are powerful testimonies to God's grace that will help you reach out to others in need. If you have found success in God's time, my prayer is that you will help others to succeed and then, together, you will ask God to transform our nations.

The great nineteenth-century preacher Charles Spurgeon wrote, 'I believe all promises of God, but many of them I have personally tried and proved. I have seen that they are true, for they have been fulfilled in me.' That is the meaning of believing and receiving. 'They have been fulfilled in me.'

As we believe and receive, we grow in faith and in spirit to become intimate friends of God. As shown in the chapter about prayers, the cause of God's acting in history is not simply his promise, but also the readiness of his people to believe, claim, and receive the promise through prayers.

God's unfailing promises are given to stimulate our belief and to motivate us to receive. *Believe and receive.*

---

158 2 Chronicles 17:9, 10, NKJV

Everything works for good

'**And we know that in all things God works for the good of those who love him.**'[159] This is a firm promise, made to us by God in the scriptures, and we can trust it completely as we move through the ups and downs of daily life. But it is a scripture that from time to time has been misunderstood, and sometimes even misquoted. So let's spend a moment unpacking what it really means.

It isn't saying that 'all things' are somehow good, even though they are painful. The God of love, beauty and tenderness does not ask us to twist our minds to believe that evil and pain can be understood as good. But he does promise to work unseen through everything that happens. He is there with us, whether we see him or not. The promise means that God can be trusted completely to bring good results even out of evil circumstances, and for this reason we do not need to fear the bad times in life.

Sometimes it is possible to see God at work but most of the time it is not easy to take it by faith that God is behind the scenes. A person could come into your life, or an event might take a turn, and you know right away that it was meant to happen. You can see that it will serve some sort of purpose, teach you or your family a lesson, or help you to figure out who you are or what you want to become. It could be a parent,

159 Romans 8:28

your long-lost friend, your roommate, neighbour or even someone you have regarded as an enemy, but when you lock eyes with that person you get a feeling maybe he or she might affect your life in some profound way.

On other occasions it can appear that God is absent, and you do not see any guiding hand to show you the way, or hear any comforting voice to help you understand what is happening. There may be times of great pain, grief, injustice or confusion. You may find yourself facing fear of what may happen in the future. And it is at these times you can look back on the scripture I have just quoted, and lean on its promise and rely on faith, hope, and trust in the Lord.

Such times have happened to us all, so I can speak from personal experience. On many occasions things have happened to me that I thought horrible, painful or unfair. But only later did I begin to understand that overcoming those bad times has helped me realise my potential, my strength, or the power of my heart and will. Knowing that God will bring good things even out of bad circumstances has instilled peace in my heart, so I have learned to be content in every situation, even though some very painful events have occurred in my life.

If you believe in God, nothing happens that puts you beyond God's reach. Make a list: illness, financial loss, sheer stupidity, love lost, love found, moments of being lost, moments of true greatness; whatever you name will test the limits of your soul. Without these trials, life would be like a smoothly paved straight flat road leading nowhere. It might be safe and comfortable, but dull and utterly pointless. God does not work on you in this way; rather he refines you in the fire, in the same way as gold is tested and purified in a furnace.

Forgive others as he forgives you

You are learning all through your life how to behave in different circumstances to reflect the love and glory that shine out of the character of God himself. To be like him is to be successful. He has promised to forgive you everything you ever did wrong if you accept his love and depend on him, and this is your true nature too. Copy him. If people hurt you, betray you or break your heart, forgive them just as the Saviour has forgiven you. And remember that doing so has helped to strengthen you in the process. You will have learned more about trusting God, and more about loving those who agitate against you. Some of the hardest and most painful lessons are the most important ones. You will have learned, for example, to be cautious about when and to whom you can open your heart.

Whether someone loves you or hates you, love that person back unconditionally, even though it may not be easy. If you achieve this, you are offering not human love but the love that comes from above. When you learn to love your enemy, you learn to see things with God's eyes and you will understand from personal experience what it is like for God, who loves you while you do not love him. He gave all he had for us when we did not even know him or give him any recognition. You are made in the image of God, so when you love people unconditionally, you are learning to be like God. How important it is to put back the lost love of God into your life!

'Everyone who loves has been born of God and knows God. Whoever does not love does not know God, because God is love.'[160]

Make every day in your life count, by appreciating and savouring every moment, and by milking from it everything you can. You may never be able to experience it again, and you do not want your time on earth to be wasted! It is good to take risks, to talk to people you have never talked to before, and to learn to be a good and careful listener. Let others experience your love, even those you have befriended who may

160 1 John 4:7

subsequently pose a threat to your spiritual, emotional, or physical well-being.

Keep your self-esteem

One of the greatest lessons you can learn from adversity is to hold your head up high, even after failure. Without experiencing failure, you would never learn the joy of victory, and your self-esteem does not depend on what you achieve, anyway. Who you really are comes from the way God sees you. He has paid the highest price of all for you – the blood of his only begotten Son – and because of that, you are infinitely precious in his sight. So, believe you are great because God lives in you, and guard your self-esteem closely. If you know that God sees you as a precious individual, then other people's low opinion will count for nothing. You can make of your life anything you wish, as long as it is within God's circle, and you can live it to the full, provided you do not leave Jesus out!

There is a Bible story that illustrates the point about self-esteem very well. There was a woman who wanted to be healed by Jesus.[161] She was an outcast, a nobody in her own culture, and she was not supposed to be out on the streets at all because she was 'unclean' from bleeding. If she had stopped to listen to the voices of those around her, she would never have made it. But her faith in Jesus was absolute, so she pressed right on through, ignoring cultural prohibitions and thick crowds, in order to get to Jesus. Significantly, it says she came up from behind to touch him. The devil will do everything he can to keep you from receiving what God has for you. But those who persist through the crowds and move forward towards God will receive what they desire most. It is not that your determination will guarantee you an easy passage, but it will guarantee you a good ending.

There is no doubt that the world is in a state of chaos, and,

161 See Luke 8:43-48

In God's time

however hard you try, you are likely to be contaminated by it. The evil in the world is like the crowds of people shouting abuse at the woman as she pushed her way through towards Jesus, trying to stop her from reaching her goal. She didn't wait to listen, and nor should you. How well you manage to charter your life through the chaotic mess depends largely on how well you rely on divine power to build your faith, your inner strength, your self-esteem and confidence.

Of course, you can attempt the passage in your own strength, and not in God's. Many people maintain a hope that they can find a way to control chaos and survive, but the scriptures explain that those who do not depend on an outer source of strength will faint before their journey is over. We are like objects that obey the laws of motion. Sir Isaac Newton's Second Law of Motion says that an object will remain in its state of rest, or continue it its state of motion, unless an external force is applied to it. This is true of human beings, too. Your life will remain just a life, static and useless, unless the force and power of Jesus acts on you. Do you want to be a passer-by or an active participant in life?

Grow slowly into your maturity

'I am sure that God, who began a good work within you, will continue his work until it is finally finished on that day when Christ Jesus comes back again.'[162] Like an artist, God has a distinctive style of his own that is repeated in everything he creates. Fruits take a whole season to mature and ripen naturally. You can spray them with CO_2 gas to make them turn red or yellow early, and they may still be edible, but the taste will never match the flavour of those left on the trees to mature naturally in God's own time. So it is with human beings. There is no satisfactory shortcut to maturity or to success. We take years to grow from being newborn babies to adulthood, and

162 Philippians 1:6, NLT

the development of our Christ-like nature is equally slow. Just as it takes years to develop a business or a career, it takes years to develop your spiritual character. If you rush it, some aspect of it will be abnormal or missing. But this is God's work. He began it when you were born, and he will bring it to completion as he has promised. So, whenever the bad times hit you, remember that God is seeing your adversity from the point of view of what he can do to develop your character, and inch it towards maturity. You have no need to fear.

There are ways of adjusting the speed of your own development just a little. You have some degree of control over what you receive from God according to your belief in him. Some people, like Moses, are able to see that God is great and all-powerful, able to save whole nations. If you see God the way Peter, Paul or John did, you will be able to do the things they did, performing miracles and bringing people to faith. Sadly, some people see God as small or untrustworthy, as did the rich young ruler[163] who was unable to trust his wealth into God's care.

All our lack of belief makes us unable to develop into what God wants us to be. We wake up with yesterday's worries and fears, weighed down by anxiety and restlessness because everything seems to depend on our own effort and we are not up to the task. We waste all our energy trying to do God's part. But Jesus says, **'My yoke is easy and my burden is light'**[164], so if we are that weighed down, we are living life the wrong way. To be successful, and to grow into maturity, we have to change our view of human beings and their size in comparison to God.

We are used to seeing adverts everywhere we go. The things that human beings have created and the services they may be able to offer are always on show, and we tend to give praise to people when we see their works. Let me turn this on its head

163 Matthew 19:21, 22
164 Matthew 11:30

for a second. Let us take a long hard look at the things God has created, and the service he is able (and willing!) to offer us, and then decide if he is not much more worthy of praise than human beings. To give recognition to God, to say aloud how big and marvellous his works really are, and to speak or sing out that he has done wonderful things is to embrace the process of worship. Since biblical times, those who have seen the wonders of God have wanted to break out in song to praise his name.

Jesus' disciples had been with him for some time already, but they were still astounded when they saw him calm a storm to save them from drowning.[165] Their reaction to such wonder was to worship him, and that should be our reaction, too. If we involve God in our affairs, he will reveal his strength and power to us, and we shall worship him.

It is not so much what happens to us in life that counts, but how we interpret those events in the light of what we know about God. The parting of the Red Sea happened both to create safe passage for the Israelites who loved God, and ultimately to destroy those who at the time were enemies of God, the Egyptians. The same lions that spared Daniel's life devoured the people who hated Daniel for worshipping God. The whale that swallowed Jonah was the very one God sent to take him to Nineveh. Forty days and nights of rain destroyed those who mocked Noah, and floated the ark that saved Noah and his family.

The message is clear – we are to wait on God, to worship him and honour him. He will protect us through desert, thorn, flood, misadventure of every kind, and even through the Valley of the Shadow of Death, until he brings us to the Heavenly City that he built himself.

---

165 Matthew 8:23-27

The most important choice

Many of us live unchecked and unexamined lives, so often failing to take full responsibility for what we believe and what we do, or bother even to wonder whether the way we lead our lives is taking us towards God or away from him. We seem instead to move from task to task, or from one job to two, or perhaps from one qualification to another, without reflecting on the larger meaning of life's purposes.

But stop and consider now what it means to drift like this so aimlessly through life. Ask yourself why you think, say and do what you do. Who taught you? Where did your ideas come from? Are you still being guided, or controlled, by what your parents did? Or the school you went to? Or the culture you grew up in? Are you still replaying past hurts, holding old grudges, and repeating ancient tunes like some broken-down record player? Whose voice is coming out of your mouth when you speak?

Unfortunately, although the details take millions of different forms, we really only have a choice of two ways of viewing the world, two 'parental' voices to copy, two role models on which to base our lives. The first may be called the secular, or humanist view. The second is God's own view. Let's take a look at the differences between them.

The secular, or humanist, belief is that every man is the

central figure in his own story, shaping events for himself, and determining the outcome he desires. The humanist believes that he is master of his own fate, that he can set limits and boundaries for himself, or choose to have none. Even his moral standards fall into the 'pick and mix' category to be selected at will, because he believes that man is intrinsically good and through education he can ultimately master the universe.

Those who follow God's view believe the opposite. They believe that only God himself can master the universe, and he alone is almighty, sovereign, and the Creator of the World. Only God is omnipotent, omnipresent, and omniscient. The moral standards he sets are for human beings to uphold and abide by for their own good. These people see God as truthful, loving, caring and personally involved in their lives, so it is a joy for them to keep his commands because they believe he is tender-hearted, merciful and can be trusted.

Now I'd like to illustrate the choice we have by telling a little story about my nephew, Tim. He was just six years old when this happened. I was phoning from the UK to my sister's house in Las Vegas, to check she had left in time to catch her flight, and also to find out her arrival time at Gatwick Airport. I hadn't seen her in twelve years, so I was really looking forward to this precious reunion. Little Tim picked up the phone, and we had a few seconds' chat before I asked if his mum was there.

'No,' he said. 'She's gone!'

'Where has she gone?' I asked

'I won't tell you,' he replied. 'I was told not to tell anyone!'

'Who said?' I pushed a little, intrigued to find out.

'My daddy,' he replied, and off he went to fetch his dad to the phone.

Well, Tim had done the right thing in obeying his father, speaking out with honesty and frankness, as only children know how. But this story prompts me to ask you, too, who told you to say what you are saying, or to do what you are doing? Which 'parental voice' are you listening to and copying? Is it the secular world ruler, Satan, or God, the Creator of the whole universe? Remember that the owner of the view you hold is the one who tells you what to say, like Tim's dad.

To be successful in God's time, you must strive to understand the difference between the two ideologies I have described above. The direction your life takes will be very different according to your belief in either viewpoint. This choice reminds me of a film I saw, in which a very brave cowboy was riding two horses at the same time. Not an easy trick at the best of times, but he succeeded because the horses were galloping very closely beside each other. Everything was fine for a minute or two, until they came up against a tree, and suddenly the cowboy was forced to choose one horse or the other; it was time to let go of something!

Jesus said, **'No one can serve two masters. Either he will hate the one and love the other, or he will be devoted to the one and despise the other. You cannot serve both God and Money.'**[166] There are the two horses, the two views of the world, and the choice we must make. Jesus recognised that money was at the heart of the secularist philosophy, and that behind it was the voice of God's enemy, dictating to everybody how to think and behave to serve his or her own selfish interests. The apostle Paul also recognised the hallmark of Satan in all the ways of the world. He reminds us, **'Our struggle is not against flesh and blood, but against the rulers, against the authorities, against the powers of this dark world and against the spiritual forces of evil in the heavenly realms.'**[167]

The only remaining weapon available to us, to help us regain our right minds, is the invitation offered to us by Jesus to fight on our behalf. We can examine where we went wrong by returning to the scriptures, and by using the weapons of light

166 Matthew 6:24
167 Ephesians 6:12

in prayer. Walking in the principles of God in every aspect of our lives connects us again to the eternal spring of spiritual joy in the love of God the Father, who has prepared for us a better life than anything afforded by this world.

The fight goes on

Now, just in case you run away with the idea that everything turns out easy from here on, let me disillusion you! I would not be telling you the truth if I left you with the impression that accepting God's view of the world and giving your life to Jesus means that you don't have to struggle any more. I can tell you from personal experience that being a Christian doesn't mean things get suddenly better. You don't have to take my word for it – a quick look inside our churches will tell you all you need to know about the ongoing battle, even in the minds of Christians.

People in church very often show up in the best clothes they can afford, sometimes just to show off. They listen to the message, the Word of God, but come away criticising the way the preacher approached the subject. And even before they have given themselves a moment to reflect on how it might impact their busy lives, their mobile phones ring and their minds are already onto a different agenda, as the people speed quickly out of church in order not to miss their friends, the football match, or the Grand Prix race on the television.

As we can see, many Christians try to ride the two horses at the same time. For some it has become normal now to eat a meal without saying grace, and morning prayer is not given its proper priority in Christian schools as it once was. People of faith are frequently tempted to pay mere lip service to God, acknowledging his existence while at the same time denying his power by living according to human traditions. We have got to the stage now of holding our Christianity as a culture and tradition, but not as a living relationship with Jesus. It is like following a god we created, instead of listening to the God who created us.

The purity of God's Word and his commands to human beings have been diluted by popular culture and what is laughably called 'political correctness'. Homosexuality, lesbianism, sexual promiscuity, child abuse, and hunger for personal power are problems the church has to face not just in the world at large but also among its own leaders. We have failed to take the problems seriously, and we have too often lost out to Satan in our homes, our communities, and even in our churches.

So the challenge exists for us all, Christians and non-Christians alike. Knowledge about God is of no use unless a personal relationship with God can elevate us to the highest moral level attainable on earth. The heavens ache for us to return to Christ, and we must be responsible for our own lives. Otherwise, we remain **'captive through hollow and deceptive philosophy'**[168] to the god of the secular world.

Jesus said, **'What good is it for a man to gain the whole world, yet forfeit his soul?'**[169] He was not just referring to those who fail to accept his precious gift of salvation, but also to those whose faith makes little or no impact on their values, and the way they conduct their lives. The scriptures make it very clear. **'Anyone who listens to the word but does not do what it says is like a man who looks at his face in a mirror and, after looking at himself, goes away and immediately forgets what he looks like.'**[170] Have you understood? The Word of God reveals the nature of God – it also reveals your own true identity if you follow what it says.

We are recognising our God-created nature when we recognise Christ. There is no neutral ground that permits a fudging of the decision we must make. There is no room for a 'maybe'. Jesus said, **'Whoever acknowledges me before men, I will also acknowledge him before my Father in heaven. But**

168 Colossians 2:8
169 Mark 8:36
170 James 1:23, 24

whoever disowns me before men, I will disown him before my Father in heaven.'[171] He is talking about adopting the character and nature of God in our earthly lives. Our problem is that we have denied our true nature, and have not wanted to be what God created us to be. God forever calls us back to recapture what we have lost, and to be known in heaven.

Jesus told a parable about a farmer sowing seed on the ground, to illustrate the different ways people respond to the Word of God.[172] I wonder if we can be honest about which group of people we fall into. First, there are those who hear about God's gift of salvation, but do not accept it. They make no effort to build their relationship with Jesus, and they are not saved. God does not want us to judge these people, or blame them for their refusal, but to let go and leave them to him.

The second group we might call the rootless Christians. They receive the Word of God with joy when they first hear it, but it doesn't stick in their hearts. Perhaps they still hold onto a wrong belief that by becoming Christians they will not have to face any further difficulties, so when hard times come their way they give up believing in God. They are not anchored in Jesus, and do not withstand trials. Jesus said, **'Not everyone who says to me, "Lord, Lord," will enter the kingdom of heaven, but only he who does the will of my Father who is in heaven.'**[173]

The third group Jesus called 'choked', referring to the way they are bound up by the constraints of earthly culture. They are people who accept the gift of salvation, and they may start by developing a relationship with Jesus. However, they are trying hard to ride two horses at once. We might call them cultural Christians, because they have a faith but don't want to give up the ways of the world. They become choked by life's worries, riches, pleasures and problems, hankering after material possessions, enslaved by debt, and weighed down by worry.

171 Matthew 10:32, 33
172 Luke 8:11-15
173 Matthew 7:21

And finally, there is a fourth group, of productive Christians. The seed that fell on good soil represents those with good and noble hearts, who receive the Word and cling to it through trials, and by persevering produce an abundant crop. They are productive because they meditate on the laws of God, and actively apply what they have learned to their ways of life. These people have truly made Christ the Lord over their whole lives – not that they are already perfect, but that they engage and struggle to reach the moral standards God sets, and the crown God has prepared for those who love him. They are on the way up, trusting wholly in Jesus. The Lord says, **'My sheep listen to my voice; I know them, and they follow me. I give them eternal life, and they shall never perish; no-one can snatch them out of my hand.'**[174]

I know many Christians whose faith is weak, and whose values and beliefs are little different from the bankrupt ones in our broken and hurting world. I can't speak for you. Only you know how Christ's words have impacted your lifestyle, or how you expect them to in the future. But what I can tell you is this – today, and every day, you must make a choice. I pray you will choose for Christ and declare, like Joshua, **'As for me and my household, we will serve the Lord.'**[175] It involves turning your life upside down. Instead of the attitude 'me first, then others, and forget about Jesus', start to live your daily life in the opposite order, by putting ***Jesus*** first, then live to serve ***Others***, and think of ***Yourself*** later. This is the godly order that pleases the Lord, and brings you ***J-O-Y***. You will see how amazingly your life will be changed, how significant and authentic you become, and what achievements you will attain.

174 John 10:27, 28
175 Joshua 24:15

A lasting peace

God's six days of creation — all the work that he put into making the world, the plants and animals that live in it, and his final masterpiece, the man and woman he made in his own likeness — was followed, significantly, by a day of rest. We call it the Sabbath, from which we get the word 'sabbatical', meaning a holiday from work.

This was God's own role model for us. He was showing us what he wanted us to do. If he can rest, so can we. God gave us rest as a gift from his own heart. Charles Bradford calls it, 'a cathedral in time, sculpted from hours and minutes, and spun out of the stuff of eternity'. The Sabbath was the seventh day, created after human beings, for the benefit of human beings. Bradford goes on, 'It pleased the Creator to make the Sabbath a vehicle for communicating his presence to his children.' And he continues, 'From the onset of human history, the Sabbath has been a gift that deepened personal relationships between God and his children.' This is clearly confirmed in the scriptures, when God spoke, saying, **'I gave them my Sabbaths as a sign between us, so they would know that I the Lord made them holy.'**[176] God did not make man for the purpose of obeying some rule about a day, but he created a day of rest, the Sabbath, to bless his people and communicate with them.

Rest is much needed, and available to every human being.

176 Ezekiel 20:12

A lasting peace

Over the centuries it has been accepted that rest is necessary and that people are healthier, happier and much more productive and fruitful when they take a day of rest every week than if they do not. In most places now such entitlement is considered normal and has been brought onto the statute books, so that employers cannot ask people to work without a break as they once could. Those who take rest appreciate it; and those who do not, for the most part, long for it. We can see it in their faces that human beings need rest. But more than mere relaxation, when used properly as time to seek God, the Sabbath not only replenishes physical strength, but also renews our spirits and lifts our souls.

The theme of rest is a central one in all the scriptures. In fact, for 'those with ears to hear' a careful reading of the Bible reveals this to be God's primary purpose for us. When God asked Moses to lead the enslaved Hebrews out from Egypt and into the Promised Land, he held out the theme and goal of rest to his people. He said, **'I will personally go with you, Moses. I will give you rest.'**[177] The ultimate threat that God used against those who rebelled against him, grumbling on the journey instead of trusting him, was, **'They shall never enter my rest.'**[178] The prophets continued on the same theme, speaking out God's desire, and his heartache that the people would not listen. **'In repentance and rest is your salvation, in quietness and trust is your strength, but you would have none of it.'**[179]

And Jesus Christ, the Son of God, was sent to earth for our sake, to show us the way. It is not surprising, then, to hear an identical message from his lips. **'Come to me, all you who are weary and burdened, and I will give you rest. Take my yoke upon you and learn from me, for I am gentle and humble in heart, and you will find rest for your souls. For my yoke is easy, and my burden is light.'**[180]

177 Exodus 33:14, NLT
178 Psalm 95:11
179 Isaiah 30:15
180 Matthew 11:28

In God's time

Finally, we have the Revelation, the last book of the Bible, in which we read, **'Blessed is the one who reads the words of this prophecy, and blessed are those who hear it and take to heart what is written in it, because the time is near.'**[181] Yes, my friend, the time is indeed near, and we cannot hold it back. Death comes to us all, and has no respect for age, wealth, position, or readiness. Now is the time to take responsibility for every remaining moment of our lives.

I believe God has blessed me and appointed me to be among his kingdom builders, and I realise I have not yet made myself fully available for what he has made me to be. I have reached the second half of my life and I can see that the music is playing much faster. Now, together, let's put aside all our earthly passions, hopes and desires, in order to be successful kingdom builders in his time. Let us run the race with patience, perseverance, and integrity, embracing it with total passion of heart, soul, mind and strength, so that we can enter God's rest in triumph.

I found this prayer somewhere, and would like to leave it with you as you reflect on all that I have written. It is entitled 'Lorica' and was attributed to St Patrick many centuries ago. Lorica is a Roman coat of armour, designed to protect the person wearing it. May this prayer, when said on your lips or read silently, serve the same purpose to your life.

I arise today through God's strength to pilot me:
God's might to uphold me, God's wisdom to guide me,
God's eye to look before me, God's ear to hear me,
God's word to speak for me, and God's hand to guard me.
Christ with me, Christ before me, Christ behind me,
Christ on my right, Christ on my left,
Christ when I lie down, Christ when I sit down,
Christ when I arise.

181 Revelation 1:3

Christ in the heart of everyone who thinks of me,
Christ in the mouth of everyone who speaks of me,
Christ in the eye that sees me, and ear that hears me.
I arise today through a mighty strength,
the invocation of the Trinity.

May God bless you, and keep you. May he be with you when you go out and come in. May the words of this book be an encouragement to you as you move forward in faith, trusting him, and at the end of it all may we meet in his rest, in his time.

Notes

Notes

Notes